VOID

Library of
Davidson College

Legal Almanac Series No. 12

LAW OF SUPPORT

THIRD EDITION

By
FRANCES W.H. KUCHLER

This Legal Almanac has been revised by the Oceana Editorial Staff

Irving J. Sloan
General Editor

**1980
Oceana Publications, Inc.
Dobbs Ferry, New York**

346.73
K95l

Library of Congress Cataloging in Publication Data

Kuchler, Frances W. H.
   Law of support.

   (Legal almanac series; no. 12)
   Includes index.
   1. Support (Domestic relations) — United States.
I. Oceana Publications, Inc. II. Title.
KF549.Z9K8   1980   346.7301'72   80-17680
ISBN 0-379-11135-7

© Copyright 1980 by Oceana Publications, Inc.

All rights reserved. No part of this publication may be reproduced or transmitted in any form or by any means, electronic or mechanical, including photocopy, recording, xerography, or any information storage and retrieval system, without permission in writing from the publisher.

Manufactured in the United States of America

82 - 7195

TABLE OF CONTENTS

Page

Chapter One
MATRIMONIAL SUPPORT 1

Chapter Two
PARENTAL SUPPORT 29

Chapter Three
PUBLIC SUPPORT 45

Appendix A
STATE-BY-STATE SUMMARY OF EFFECT OF
DIVORCE ON MATRIMONIAL SUPPORT 67

Appendix B
RIGHT OF DOWER, CURTESY AND
STATUTORY SUBSTITUTIONS 75

Appendix C
LIMIT OF VALUE OF HOMESTEAD 79

Appendix D
REVISED UNIFORM RECIPROCAL ENFORCE-
MENT OF SUPPORT ACT (1968) 83

Appendix E
SAMPLE SEPARATION AGREEMENT 97

Appendix F
SUPPORT OF PAUPER RELATIVES 105

Appendix G
FORM: AGREEMENT TO FURNISH SUPPORT .. 107

Appendix H
FORM: AGREEMENT BETWEEN PARENT AND
CHILD FOR SUPPORT 111

Appendix I
FORM: AGREEMENT BETWEEN PARENT AND
CHILD FOR SUPPORT-CONVEYANCE OF REAL
PROPERTY AS CONSIDERATION 113

Appendix J
FORM: AGREEMENT BETWEEN PARENT AND CHILD FOR SUPPORT-TRANSFER OF PERSONAL PROPERTY AS CONSIDERATION .. 114

Appendix K
FORM: AGREEMENT BETWEEN PARENT AND CHILD FOR SUPPORT-PARENT TO PROVIDE FOR CHILD IN WILL AS CONSIDERATION 115

Index 117

Series Conversion Table 119

Chapter I

MATRIMONIAL SUPPORT

The Obligation to Support

It is common knowledge that a man has an obligation to support his wife, as well as his minor children. There are few people who have not heard of the Domestic Relations, or Family Court, wherein proceedings against a negligent husband may result in an order to pay a suitable amount to his wife and children if he has been lax in his duty to provide for them. The procedure in these courts is simple; if complainant wives do not have their own attorneys these will be furnished by the court.

Desertion: Every state in the United States has a statute applicable to this obligation. The man who deserts his family, without justification, and leaves them in a destitute condition is subject to criminal as well as civil liability. The severity of the sentence varies in different states; fines range from one hundred to one thousand dollars and jail terms may be from one to several years in duration. Desertion, often described as "wilful neglect," is classified by the criminal laws as a misdemeanor or even a felony, a felony being a more serious crime. The MAINE statute defines desertion as a felony if it is of a "high and aggravated" nature and as a misdemeanor when it is not so regarded. The penalty for the felony, for instance, in MAINE is a fine of not more than five hundred dollars and not more than two years in prison, or both. For the misdemeanor it is a fine of not more than three hundred dollars and not more than eleven months in prison or both.

By the usual court procedure, the husband may be permitted to post a bond as a guarantee that he will pay the amount that the court has ordered for the support of his family and thereby escape the criminal penalties. This is naturally a more practical solution to the problem and is therefore much more frequent than actual commitment. The court has many circumstances to consider in the determination of cases of this sort; the extent and availability of the wife's means, their children, and her possible pregnancy are important factors. Some states have statutes which specifically provide for the desertion of a pregnant wife and the penalties which these describe are more severe than for cases of ordinary desertion.

As in the case of all crimes, there are defenses to the crime of desertion. A husband may be excused from supporting his wife where she has given him good grounds for divorce according to the laws of the state in which they live, or if she has abandoned him for no justifiable cause. A divorce or a separation agreement whose terms are complied with are other adequate defenses. If the husband can prove his "inability" or inadequacy because of illness or infirmity, he is also excused from the duty of supporting his wife.

From reading the desertion and non-support statutes one might be inclined to assume that, since there were strict laws on the subject, there could not be very many cases in which families of wives and children were left destitute if the husband were employed. As a matter of fact, however, desertion is one of the most serious of our social and economic problems. Figures of the Social Security Administration show that 63% of the families who were receiving aid to dependent children were those in which the father was absent from the home. This figure does not take into account the children who were living in foster homes because of their father's absence or the number of families on home relief for the same reason.

Enforcement of Support: The legal means of enforcement is complicated by the fact that it is usually very difficult to serve a summons or warrant of arrest on a man in order to bring him into court. (Even when he is actually before the court he may successfully conceal his assets or earning abilities. In large cities there are so many cases of this sort that there is not sufficient time or means for courts to give each case the attention it deserves.) The greater number of men who desert their families go into other states in order to avoid their responsibilities. Unless a wife is in a fairly advantageous financial position she cannot hire a detective or an attorney to assist her with her problem. There are various agencies[1] which are active in this sort of work; the National Desertion Bureau in New York City has been extremely successful in "tracking down" errant husbands and in obtaining assistance for deserted wives. This organization is a charitable one and only handles cases for clients who are entirely unable to afford a private attorney

Recently there have been *uniform state support laws* enacted which might prove valuable in reducing the number of families who are public charges because of a deserting parent. These laws make it possible for a dependent wife to state her case to the court of the state in which the husband resides without being personally present.

In order to do this, she must present her case to the family or domestic relations court where she resides. The judge of that court will then forward her verified petition with all of the facts, and will certify that the summons, which has been issued out of his court for the defendant, has been returned with an affidavit to the effect that such defendant could not be located. The judge of the second court (which has jurisdiction over the husband) will then issue a summons out of his court and fix a time and place for a hearing. If the defendant denies the statements in the wife's petition, the proceedings will be halted until both courts have sufficient proof of all of the facts. The complainant wife is represented in the second court by a state's attorney or similar officer. In this way, testimony and evidence are passed back and forth between the courts until a final decision has been reached. The second court,

---

[1] There are state agencies for locating deserting husbands, but in general these do not have sufficient funds to be very effective.

if the husband has been found to be at fault, will then order him to make payments, which will be forwarded to the first court where they will be duly given to the wife.

Today, every state has adopted either the Uniform Support of Dependants Act or Uniform Reciprocal Enforcement of Support Act, amplifying the procedure to compel support of dependents whose responsible relatives are in other states.

These laws are *civil laws* and not criminal laws. There are good social and psychological reasons why it is not considered advantageous to the family relationship to regard a deserting husband as a criminal. (There is an earlier group of uniform desertion laws which were criminal and which applied criminal means to enforce the husband's liability.)

Mutual Obligation: What of the wife's obligation toward her husband for support? The marriage relation, or "status" as it is known legally, imposes a duty on both parties. Sometimes the states deal specifically with this duty and sometimes it is included in statutes having broader applications, such as those defining the obligations of various members of the family toward their pauper relatives. CALIFORNIA provides that a wife must support her husband out of her separate property if he is unable to care for himself, or is infirm. (MONTANA and OKLAHOMA have statutes on the subject of marriage obligations which state that both spouses owe each other respect, fidelity and support.) The husband must support the wife, but if he is unable to do so she must assist him. NORTH and SOUTH DAKOTA have similar provisions. COLORADO, IOWA and others state that there is a joint liability of husband and wife for the support of the family and that family expenses are chargeable upon the property of both. In these states the spouses can be sued jointly to recover expenses incurred by others.

Extent of the Obligation: There are many people who may be interested in the extent and kind of support which those responsible must give to their families. Is a husband obligated to give over all of his earnings to his wife and children, or is this a matter for his personal determination? The Desertion Statutes say that a man cannot leave his family in necessitious or destitute circumstances, but as a practical matter, just what does this mean? The courts of all of the states generally agree that a husband is liable for his wife's necessaries, and that he is also liable to third persons who supply her with these necessaries when he fails to do so. The same liability applies to those responsible for the care of minor children.

What are "necessaries" to a wife and family must be determined from the circumstance of each particular case, as a court usually finds that the customary mode of living is the yardstick by which the amount of support is measured. However, there are some general rules which have been followed in this matter. "Necessaries" to a family always include: household furniture, rent, clothing, groceries, heating, cooking, laundry, education of the children and medical care. Included in the circumstances which excuse a husband from his liabilities toward the support of his wife are her "misconduct," that is, generally, adultery on her part. Some courts hold, nevertheless, that a husband must pay his wife's medical expenses whatever the cause of their living separately may be. Legal expenses are a necessary, sometimes even when the wife is at fault.

There are many instances where a wife has an income from her own separate property, or is carrying on a business which would be adequate to support her and her children. If such a wife can and does contract for her own necessaries, then she is personally liable for them, but if she does not, the husband remains liable even though the wife could afford to pay her own expenses. This duty of the husband is a fundamental one and arises from the marriage relationship itself, although there may be cases in which a valid agreement between husband and wife may allow for modifications of this rule. A husband is liable for his wife's premarital debts only to the extent of property which he acquired from her by reason of the marriage.

Uniform Desertion and Non-Support Acts: The Uniform Desertion and Non-Support Act has now been adopted by the following jurisdictions:

ALABAMA	NEW JERSEY
ALASKA	NORTH DAKOTA
CALIFORNIA	OKLAHOMA
DELAWARE	SOUTH DAKOTA
HAWAII	TEXAS
IDAHO	UTAH
ILLINOIS	VERMONT
KANSAS	VIRGINIA
MASSACHUSETTS	WASHINGTON
MISSISSIPPI	WISCONSIN
NEVADA	WEST VIRGINIA
NEW HAMPSHIRE	WYOMING

It is the general rule in the states in which these acts are effective that divorce does not relieve the father from support of his minor children. However, where the decree awards exclusive custody to the wife, the husband cannot be found guilty of wilful desertion of the child. In those cases where the wife deserts the husband without reasonable cause, he cannot be held liable for her support. Where the separation is a voluntary one, the husband's obligation to support his wife continues. In all cases of support it must be shown that there is ability to support. If the husband is unable to support his wife and minor children, because of illness or inability to find employment, he cannot be convicted under the desertion statutes.

Property Rights of a Wife

At the present time, one is so accustomed to the fact that a wife may hold property as well as her husband that few may realize that this was not always true. A series of laws, which were first enacted in England in the nineteenth century and more recently in all of our states, known as the

"Married Women's Property Acts," first made it possible for a married woman to hold property without her husband's interest and control. Our states, therefore, always have a particular statute defining the "separate property" of a married woman and her rights, interests and liabilities.

MISSOURI, for example, defines the "separate property" of a married woman as: "all the real and personal property belonging to her at the time of the marriage or coming to her during the marriage by gift, bequest or inheritance, or purchase with her separate means or out of her separate labor, together with the income and profits thereof." This is her sole property and under her sole control. MISSISSIPPI states that marriage shall not impose any disabilities on a woman with regard to the ownership and disposition of her property. NEW JERSEY uses broader terms, that is, a married woman's separate property includes property which she receives or obtains in any manner after her marriage. Some states provide for the recording of the wife's separate personal property in the office of the county recorder, so that there will be no possible confusion over her title to it.

Formerly, when husband and wife were considered legally as one person, the husband being "the one," a wife could not make any contracts by herself. This theory is still apparent in five states which do not permit a wife to contract regarding her real estate without her husband's consent. In TEXAS, the signature of the husband is necessary for the conveyance and encumbrance, such as mortgaging, of her own real estate, and is also required for the transfer of her stocks and bonds. In ALABAMA, FLORIDA, INDIANA, NORTH CAROLINA, likewise, a husband must join in his wife's contracts to sell or mortgage her own land.

Generally, the Married Women's Property Acts of all of the states provide that a wife's property shall not be liable for the debts of her husband. There may, however, be some slight modification of this rule, such as the VER-

MONT law which makes the annual products of the wife's property liable for the debts of the husband which were created because of the purchase of necessaries for his wife and family or for the improvement of her separate real estate. Her property is liable for family expenses only in those states where it is expressly stated that the property of both is charged with the expenses of the family and children. In such cases, the statute usually limits the wife's liability to reasonable and necessary family expenses and education of the children.

Included in a wife's separate property are her earnings. These may be acquired by reason of a regular wage earning position or by means of a business venture. In the latter event the wife may contract solely, without her husband's consent, in her own business matters, even in those states where she may not convey land without his consent. In TEXAS, however, a wife must, with the consent of her husband, petition the court for the purpose of becoming a "femme sole" (single woman) to carry on her own business or trade.

The word "earnings" has been variously interpreted by the courts. That is, money earned inside the home or in connection with a husband's business is often considered as a part of the husband's property and not that which belongs solely to the wife.

If a wife is a wage-earner, she is now entitled to her own damages where such are recovered in an action for personal injuries. If the husband has paid the medical expenses, he may claim reimbursement out of the damage award, in addition to his damages for the loss of her "consortium" (or companionship). There is no such comparable action permitted to the wife. As most of our states now have Workmen's Compensation laws, we may add that a compensation award for injuries to a wife who is employed belongs solely to the wife, and not to her husband.

Community Property

Do our laws define the separate property of a husband

as well as that of a wife? In addition to the Married Women's Property Acts there have been other statutory changes which alter the common law rule whereby all property ownership was vested in the husband. There are at present twelve so-called "Community Property" states. In these states all property which does not specifically belong to either the husband or the wife is community property which is, in a broad sense, owned by both of them.

Historically, this system did not originate in England as most of our American laws, but was a part of the Civil law of Spain, and was first introduced here in those states whose territory was once in Spanish possession; that is: ARIZONA, CALIFORNIA, LOUISIANA, NEVADA, NEW MEXICO and TEXAS. IDAHO and WASHINGTON copied their earlier statutes on this subject from the CALIFORNIA laws. MICHIGAN, NEBRASKA, OKLAHOMA and OREGON have recently adopted this system, principally for purposes of taxation, so that the tax burden may be divided between the spouses.

NEBRASKA became a community property state by laws effective on September 7, 1947. Definitions from these laws may be used as a general example of what is meant by community ownership. The separate property of a husband is here defined as:

"All property of the husband both real and personal, owned or claimed by him before marriage or before September 7, 1947, whichever is later, and that acquired afterwards by gift, devise, or descent or received as compensation for personal injuries, shall be his separate property."

The separate property of the wife is similarly defined.

Community or common property is:

"All property acquired by either the husband or wife during marriage and after September 7, 1947, except that which is the separate property of either shall be deemed the community or common property of the husband and wife, and each shall be vested with an undivided one half interest therein; and all the effects which the husband and wife possess at the time the marriage may be dissolved shall be regarded as common effects or gains unless the contrary be satisfactorily proved."

The management and control of the various properties defined is stated thus by the NEBRASKA Law:

> "The wife shall have the management and control and may dispose of her separate property, both real and personal, and that portion of the common or community property consisting of her earnings, all rents, interest, dividends, and other income from her separate property, and all other common or community property, the title to which stands in her name. The husband shall have the management and control and may dispose of his separate property, both real and personal, and all community property, the management, control and disposition of which is not conferred upon the wife hereby."

Simply stated, after September 7, 1947, NEBRASKA regards all property of a husband and wife not specified as the separate property of either, as belonging to them both in equal shares. (The property which they hold in common is thereby liable for the debts of both or either of them unless such debts can be proven to have been contracted in the course of acquiring, holding or managing the community property which stands in the name of one of them. Then, this particular portion of property alone is liable for that debt.)

On the dissolution of a marriage in NEBRASKA each spouse has a vested half interest in the community property, although the court may at its discretion divest one spouse of a part or all of his share. On the death of husband or wife, the other may administer the common property in the same manner as may the surviving partner in a partnership.

All of the community property states make the husband the spouse controlling the common property, but in some states his control is limited. The most important limit is his incapacity to sell or encumber the real estate without his wife's signature (joinder), although generally he may dispose of the personal property without her consent. However, there can be no such conveyance which would defraud the wife of her interest in the community property.

At the death of the husband the wife assumes the role of an equal, since she becomes the owner of her share of the community property, of which half is now under her control. The half which belonged to the husband, if he has not disposed of it by his Will, may go to his descendants, or it may go to the wife. The states vary in this respect.

Neither spouse has testamentary disposition of more than his (or her) half of the common property. If such an attempt is made, the other spouse may elect to take this share against the Will.

Among the territories, HAWAII and PUERTO RICO have the community property system.

Marriage Settlements

The fundamental duty of a husband to support his wife may be altered by an agreement between the parties. These contracts will be recognized as valid by the courts only if both parties had capacity to understand the nature of the agreement and if the contract was not brought about by undue influence or fraud. They will be set aside if the court finds that they are unfair to either party, or against public policy.

The consideration for such a contract is the marriage itself; if the marriage does not take place the contract will not come into effect. A common form of marriage settlement is an agreement on the part of the wife to release her rights in her husband's property in exchange for a deed to property of adequate value.

Rights of a Surviving Spouse

Dower and Curtesy: At common law dower and curtesy were the names given to the interests of the surviving spouse in the lands owned by the deceased spouse. Dower was the right of the widow, and it consisted of the income from *one third* of her husband's real property during her life. In case of absolute divorce and other circumstances she could be deprived of this right.

Curtesy was the widower's right to a life estate in *all* of his deceased wife's lands. However, it was necessary for a living child to have been born of the marriage before the husband could obtain the right of curtesy. At common law although dower was not effective until the husband's death, curtesy was an interest which existed during the marriage.

In the United States there are at present many variations of common law dower and curtesy. A few of the states have retained them both as they were, but the majority of states have either abolished one or the other, or altered their extent. As may be seen from Appendix B curtesy has largely been abolished. "Dower," however, is now sometimes used in reference to the husband as well as the wife, and grants him a third or, in some states, a half, of the income from the deceased's real estate for his life. In a few states, such as FLORIDA, dower is more than an interest for life being an absolute ownership in a portion of the deceased husband's lands. In addition to an interest in real estate, ownership of personal property is sometimes included in dower.

There are several means by which dower may be defeated. A property settlement between husband and wife may take the place of her dower right. They may contract with each other as to the rights of each in the property of the other, and if this contract is fair, it will be upheld by the courts. Where the wife abandons the husband without just cause, or is divorced from him because of her "misconduct," she forfeits her dower.

Dower may be barred by Will. Unless a Will clearly and expressly states that the widow (or widower) is to have both dower and the property indicated by the Will, it is understood that the provision in the Will takes the place of dower. In all but a few states, the surviving spouse, if dissatisfied with the terms of the Will, is permitted to make an election to take dower instead of the testamentary disposition. The election must be filed with the court within a certain period of time, usually six months after the Will has been offered for probate. Where there is no statutory provision for dower, the dissatisfied spouse may elect to take property determined by the laws covering the situation where the deceased leaves no Will.

These laws of "intestate succession" (which come into effect when the decedent has left no Will) vary in the different states. However, they all depend upon the closeness of the relationship of those surviving to the deceased person. Generally, a spouse or children take precedence over other relatives.

Homestead: Another statutory departure from the common law rule vesting all marital property in the husband is that known as the "homestead exemption." This idea also originated in the Republic of TEXAS, in 1839. The homestead is a piece of real estate whose value and size is limited by statute, which is specifically set aside as the family home. It is protected by law from attachment by most creditors.

The husband, as the head of the family, is usually given the right to select the homestead, but the wife may be so empowered where the husband has failed to do so. It may be selected from the separate real estate of either husband or wife or, in community property states, from the common property of the marriage. Any person who is the head of a family is entitled to a homestead in most states.

In addition to freedom from liability for most debts, the most important feature of the homestead laws is the protection of this property from destruction by one of the spouses. A husband and wife must join in any conveyance thereof, or openly agree to abandon it as a homestead. One spouse may not bar the other, or the children of the marriage, from the use of the premises, except in those cases of divorce or separation where it has been given to one of the parties by order of a court. Upon the death of husband or wife, the survivor has a vested interest in the homestead. This may be a life estate in the whole property, which descends to the decedent's heirs upon the death of the surviving spouse, or it may be an interest in fee absolute. In any event, the survivor is protected from deprivation of the homestead by testamentary disposal; if an attempt has been made to will it away, the remaining spouse may elect to take against the Will. Where no homestead has been selected before death, in community property states the court will select a "probate homestead" out of the community property.

A list of limits on homestead values appears in Appendix C. As may be seen, these values were formulated years ago and the laws on this subject have been modernized. Consequently the original purpose of the law, that is, to insure a dwelling for a widow, probably does not apply in very many cases today. Dwelling places in the amount of two thousand dollars, including improvements, are rare. However, the stated amount is protected even though the total property has to be sold for the payment of debts. A few of our states such as FLORIDA and KANSAS, have no limit on the value of the homestead, although the acreage may be limited. In KANSAS a homestead is defined as: "160 acres outside or one acre inside the limits of an incorporated city which is used as a residence at the time of one spouse's death."

Family Allowances: The laws of a number of states have given further consideration to the support of a surviving spouse by minor allowances out of the deceased's estate to the surviving spouse and children. These allowances generally cannot be defeated by Will, and become charges upon the estate, whether thereby it is solvent or not. Sometimes they are subject to funeral and administration expenses. Some states provide for this support by the setting apart of personal property, in addition to recognizing the right of the family to certain articles such as household furniture and clothing.

Maintenance is usually provided for the family in this manner for a certain limited time, six months to a year in most cases.

Effect of Divorce, Annulment or Separation on Support*

Divorce

Although the Domestic Relations and Family Courts are qualified to assist a family in obtaining support from the father or parent, these courts do not have the power to grant divorces, separations or annulments. Divorce actions are brought in a higher court. These, like other court actions, must be begun by the service of a summons upon the other party. When a wife (or husband) receives such a summons she must answer it properly. Therefore it is important for her to obtain the services of a competent attorney immediately. In most of our large cities there are Legal Aid Societies which will assist her in defending the action or will refer her to an attorney, if she has insufficient funds with which to retain one. Local Bar Associations are also helpful in these matters, and have referral lists of attorneys who have volunteered their services at reasonable fees.

If, on the other hand, she wishes to obtain a divorce she must ascertain whether there are sufficient grounds upon which to base her action. These same associations will give assistance or advice to a complainant as well as to a defendant party.

Let us assume that the divorce action has been completed in the proper legal manner and an absolute divorce decree has been handed down by the court. Thus, that which was once a valid existing marriage is now dissolved.

At the present time there are many causes in our country for which a divorce may be granted. These include: adultery, desertion, insanity, neglect, drunkenness, physical and mental cruelty, and others. These causes play a part in the court's decision regarding final distribution of the property of the parties and in the award of alimony to either of them. Formerly in England, when the Ecclesi-

---

* See also *Law of Separation and Divorce*, by Parnell J.T. Callahan, Legal Almanac Series, Vol. 1.

astical Courts had charge of the matters, alimony was merely the enforcement of the husband's fundamental duty to support his wife, and therefore the term "alimony" could not mean anything other than a payment to the wife. It was, at that time, a money judgment against the husband and was payable in installments.

Alimony

In all except a few states and territories of the United States, a wife who is successful in an action for a divorce or a separation is allowed "alimony" and in most states, her Court costs and counsel fees as well. For a long period of time a wife who was granted an annulment received no alimony on the theory that the marriage, having been voided, never existed, whether it had been void from the beginning or merely voidable at the option or election of the injured or defrauded spouse. In recent years, however, many states have begun to allow the award of alimony to a wife whose marriage has been annulled provided she acted in good faith and otherwise was in a meritorious position. If for example, a wife married her husband, believing that he was free to marry, whereas, in fact, a prior divorce obtained by the husband, was invalid, the wife may be awarded alimony even though her marriage was void from the start since the husband had an existing marriage in effect at the time he and the wife participated in their ceremony of marriage.

The word "alimony" is derived from the latin "alimonia," meaning sustenance. "Alimony" therefore is the sustenance, maintenance or support which the wife receives from her divorced husband. It stems from the common law right of the wife to be supported by her husband and to be nourished or sustained by him.

In the majority of states, there is legislation and there are statutes in effect giving the Court discretion to make an allowance for the support of the wife and the children not only permanently, and in the judgment of divorce, but "pendente lite," or during the pendency and carrying on of the law suit. This allowance is made not only to permit the wife to maintain the action if she has a reasonable ground or reasonable chance of succeeding, but also to keep her and the children from becoming public charges. In a few states, the husband, if disabled or necessitous is allowed alimony from the property or earnings of the wife, but such instances are comparatively rare, and as a rule are limited to cases where if the wife does not furnish some support for the husband, he is likely to become a public charge, or to cases where the wife's income and assets were derived from the husband or as a result of the husband's efforts.

While the word "alimony" strictly speaking, refers only to support or sustenance for the wife, it is generally used to include both payments for the benefit of the wife which strictly speaking are "alimony," and payments for the benefit of the children, which are known colloquially as "child support." Some judgments of divorce provide for the payment of "alimony" for the support of the wife and the minor children, while others provide for one periodic payment for the wife, to be made weekly or monthly, and another payment for the children. The allocation of the total amount of support to be paid to the wife is quite important, since the husband is allowed a tax deduction on monies paid solely for the support of the wife, while the wife must pay the tax on that sum. However, if there is a separate sum to be paid for the support of the children, the husband is required to pay the income tax on that amount, and the wife receives it tax-free albeit for the benefit of the children. Under some circumstances, it is possible for the parties, if they agree upon the requirements of the wife and the children, to allocate the payments to be paid to the wife between "alimony" and "child support," to lessen the tax impact by splitting the burden of the income tax and thus leaving more money available for support and less to be paid in taxes.

Alimony after a trial and in the final judgment is known merely as "alimony" or as "permanent alimony." Alimony awarded after the action has been started, but before it has been tried, is known variously as a "allowance," "temporary allowance," "temporary alimony," "alimony pendente lite," or "allowance pending trial." Alimony after the trial is generally referred to as "alimony" or "permanent alimony."

There are some states where no alimony is allowed, on the theory that once a marriage is dissolved, it is dissolved for all purposes. Notable among these states are Texas and Pennsylvania. Alimony is largely discretionary, and the exercise of judicial discretion may at times surprise layman who merely rely on the words of the statute. As a rule, the Courts take into consideration all of the factors involved, including the husband's means, the husband's salary, the husband's earning ability, if he is not living up to his potentiality, or if he is obviously keeping his income low for alimony purposes, the amount of his capital, the amount of the wife's earning ability, the obligations of the wife to care for the children, which may leave her no time or no opportunity for gainful employment, the wife's earning ability and the wife's assets.

Until a few years ago, the law in many states provided for the husband to support the wife in accordance with the husband's means and earning ability honestly exercised, whether the wife happened to be a millionnaire or a pauper. In recent years, however, Courts have taken a more realistic view, and the present tendency is for the Court to take into consideration the monies and capital available to the wife.

Also important and considered by the Courts, is the standard of living to which the parties were accustomed, and their station in life. If the parties lived beyond their means, and if they maintained their standard of living only by a continuous invasion of capital, the Court trying the case or hearing the testimony of the parties, may, in its discretion, direct that alimony be paid only out of income and without regard to the capital assets involved.

While the Courts in community property states are empowered to make divisions of community property, they usually do so without compelling either party to lose title to his or her separate property. Some states permit a Court to award to one spouse some portion of the capital assets of the other spouse, but these states are in the minority. The circumstances of the particular case may be controlling and you are warned to consult your attorney with respect to any difficult questions and to make a full disclosure to your attorney of your means and assets.

In some states, the Court may award the wife a lump sum, in lieu of periodic and installment payments which otherwise might be directed. The Court may even invade the capital of the husband to have him pay certain bills and charges, particularly medical expenses incurred or to be incurred by an ill or needy wife or children or to pay educational expenses. In almost all states, the Courts have the power to regulate the occupancy of jointly owned real property and in some states have the right and power to direct a transfer of title. In some instances, the Court in a final judgment of divorce may restore to each party all property not otherwise disposed of which either party acquired from the other party during marriage.

As a general rule, where the husband sues his wife for a divorce, and obtains a divorce, the wife does not receive permanent alimony although Courts have wide discretion in this regard. In some cases the Courts may even direct a wife who is divorced for her own misconduct to pay alimony to a husband, and, in "balancing the equities, and in taking into consideration the length of time the marriage has lasted, the conduct of the parties over a period of years, the number of children born of the marriage, and the means of both parties, as well as the station in life of the parties and the standard of living to which the parties and the children have become accustomed."

Where a husband sues his wife for divorce, and obtains a judgment of divorce, the wife as a rule does not receive permanent alimony. In any event, however, if she shows a necessity for support pending the trial, she usually is allowed temporary alimony, and, where the husband institutes the action, the wife is almost always allowed counsel fees. In most instances, the counsel fees of the wife are charged to the husband, and he may be directed by the Court either in a temporary order, or in the final judgment of divorce or separation or even in the judgment of annulment, to pay counsel fees for the wife.

Where separation agreements are worked out, the counsel fees are subject to agreement by the parties and their attorneys. As a rule, the parties follow the prevailing law as enunciated by the Courts in contested matrimonial cases, and both the amount of counsel fees, and their incidence and the determination of the spouse who pays them, are computed in accordance with the money available to both parties.

Enforcement and Modification of Alimony Awards

A judgment or decree which makes an award of alimony may be enforced by one or more proceedings. While the most commonly encountered enforcement procedure is a motion or application to the Court which granted the judgment to punish the offending husband (or in the rare cases where a wife is directed to pay alimony or support or where the wife refuses to permit the husband to see the children, the offending wife) for contempt of Court for failure to comply with the judgment. "Contempt" is a most drastic remedy, and as a rule will be invoked only if the decree awarding the alimony cannot be enforced either by sequestration (seiquire of the defendant's property), or by reduction of the provisions of the decree to a money judgment and execution by the sheriff or marshal against the husband's property.

Money Judgment

If the spouse (usually the husband) who has been directed to pay alimony has not compiled with the divorce decree, it may be easier and less costly for the wife to ask the Court to give her a money judgment against the husband. This money judgment may then be "docketed" or filed not only in the county in which the divorce was granted, but in any county in the State. It then becomes a "lien" on any real property or real estate owned by the defendant, and the property cannot be sold without satisfying the lien. Where the husband has left the state, but owns real property in the State, this is most effective. Likewise, if he maintains a bank account, or a business, or owns stock or bonds which are held by a bank or custodian, or which are in the temporary possession or custody of the wife, the money judgment will permit the sheriff or marshall to levy on the property, and to satisfy the arrears out of the property. The real property of the defendant may likewise be sold at auction by the sheriff, and the judgment satisfied from the proceeds.

Garnishee

In the usual case of a judgment, a garnishee of the defendant or debtor's earnings or income is permitted only up to ten percent of his property. Since a man earning $100.00 a week, and directed to pay $40.00 a week alimony would pay only $10.00 a week, as opposed to $40.00, a garnishee in and of itself would not be particularly effective. However, the tendency has been to permit the Court to make an order, on notice to the defendant's employer, ordering the employer to deduct from the defendant's wages the amount of alimony and to forward this alimony directly to the wife. This in effect relieves the wife of the necessity of running after the husband, and as long as he is steadily employed, and does not lose his job, the judgment will be effective. In some cases, however, the entry of such an order may result in the defendant being discharged, and a wife should exercise supreme caution before taking this step.

Sequestration

If a husband cannot be found, or if he can be found, but refuses to make payment, and the wife does not want to have him jailed for contempt of court, an alternative method is the "sequestration" of his property. In most states, an application to punish for contempt will not be entertained or heard by the Court or will not be granted by the Court unless the wife can swear that sequestration of property would have no effect, or that the property has been so hidden and secreted that it cannot be located.

In the usual case of sequestration, if the husband has income producing property, stocks, bonds and automobile, jewelry and bank accounts, the wife may apply to the Court for the appointment of a receiver. Sometimes she herself will be appointed the receiver while on other occasions the Court will appoint some unbiased and disinterested third party. The receiver, when appointed, must file a bond to insure his faithful compliance with his duties. He is then empowered to seize the property and from the proceeds of the property, to pay the wife, the amount which is due to her for her support and the support of the children.

The receiver is paid a percentage of the amount which he receives and pays out and he is held strictly accountable.

In some cases, where the delivery of the property to the receiver is resisted, the receiver may be required to retain an attorney to enforce his position as receiver.

This adds to the expense and leaves less money available for the wife, and less money available for return to the husband in the event of the satisfaction of the wife's claim without the exhaustion of the fund or property seized by or delivered to the receiver.

Security for Future Payment

Where the husband has hidden his property or where he has no visible property, but there has been no change in his circumstances in the time which has elapsed after the entry of the judgment directing the payment of the alimony, the Court may order him to show why he should not be punished for contempt of Court. If the Court finds that he is capable of making the payments, and that he has not suffered any reverses or losses since the date of the hearing at which the alimony was fixed, he will be adjudged in contempt of Court and will be fined the amount of his arrears and possibly an additional amount as a penalty. As a rule, the amount of the fine is fixed at the amount of his arrears and he is directed to pay the fine, sometimes in weekly installment in addition to current alimony, and sometimes in one lump sum or four or five lump sums over a period of time. As a rule, additional attorney's fees will be awarded to the wife and the husband in addition to being required to pay the amount of alimony, will also be required to pay more fees to the wife's attorneys.

When the husband is found guilty of contempt of Court, the order punishing him for contempt usually provides that if he does not make the payment directed in the finding order, he may be arrested and placed in jail. The usual jail sentence is three months for payments under $500.00 and six months for payments of over $500.00. The sentences vary, however, and these terms are by no means universal.

While contempt is a drastic remedy, and as a rule will not be imposed unless there has been a clear showing of wilful conduct as opposed to mere inability to pay, the wife should be cautious about asking for such relief. While the husband is in jail, his payments will be suspended for the period of his incarceration, and need not be made up after his release. The wife, by putting her husband or former husband in jail, may in effect be "killing the goose that lays the golden egg." She may be better advised to enter a money judgment, and to get as much as she can, in the meantime waiting for the husband's fortunes to improve, on the theory that half a loaf is better than none.

If a husband has disposed of his property, or if at the time of the trial he had stocks and bonds worth $10,000.00 but three months later has none, he must offer a satisfactory explanation of his reverses. By the same theory, if the husband has quit his job, and cannot show a medical necessity for ceasing his employment, the Court will presume that he has done so without any adequate justification and the husband may be held guilty of contempt of Court. As a rule, a husband will be directed to pay alimony and child support in accordance with his means and with his earning ability honestly exercised. A man capable of earning $150.00 a week who takes a job at $50.00 a week, may nevertheless be directed to pay $75.00 a week alimony if the Court finds that he wilfully and without a valid reason rejected employment permitting him to make more money. The same applies to a husband who for no apparent reason decides to stop work and to take life a little easier. The Court may compel him either to work at an adequate salary if a position is obtainable, or will incarcerate him if he does not work and does not attempt to obtain employment commeasurate with his ability.

In almost every case, it becomes a question of the husband's good faith, and the Court will usually hold a hearing. In some states, such as New York, husbands may be jailed without a hearing, but the general tendency is against any such incarceration without an actual trial or hearing of live witnesses, as opposed to a determination on papers.

Alimony Jails

In almost all states, a husband who has been guilty of wilful defaults and who has been held in contempt of court will be placed in alimony jail. In some states he is placed in the County Jail while in other states there is a civil jail, as distinguished from a criminal jail, where he is confined, but is not confined at hard labor. However, in the words of an elderly publisher whose young third wife succeeded in having him committed to jail, "While the warden treated me well, jail is still jail."

Modification of Alimony Awards

If the husband loses his job, or if he suffers reverses and illness which decrease his earning potential, he may apply to the Court for a modification, reduction or postponement of the amounts of payments directed by the decree. He may make this application at any time there is a substantial change in his circumstances.

By the same token, if the needs of the wife and the children increase, by reason of accident, illness or because the children grow older and require more money, the wife may ask the Court to increase the amount. If the husband's circumstances improve and he earns more money, the wife may ask that she and the children be permitted to share in his affluence, to improve their own standard of living. Typical examples of circumstances permitting increase are serious illness or accident suffered by one of the children requiring special care, illness or disability of the wife or of one of the children, interfering with the wife making a living, or the inheritance by the husband of a large sum of money or his obtaining a new position at a vastly increased income.

Custody: If there are any children of the marriage, their custody must be provided for during the suit as well as after the divorce. In both cases, this is entirely a matter for the courts' discretion, and the state laws are always worded to that effect. There is no law in any state which makes it a rule for the children to remain with either the husband or the wife during a divorce action or afterwards.

When the wife had no property rights, and few other rights, the father was always considered the proper guardian for the child in any event. Now it is sometimes customary for very small children to be placed in the care of their mother even though they may later live with their father. The courts are expected to consider all of the circumstances of the case and place the children where they will be most adequately cared for. It must be added that there are times when neither parent is deemed fit to have the children in its custody, and they are then given to other relatives or even strangers.

In the majority of cases the custody of children is given to the mother. In some cases even the mother who is decreed by the court to be the party at fault may still be considered the most suitable person to have the custody of the children. The order of the court regarding custody during and after suit is always subject to change at the court's discretion. There is never a final decree on custody.

Annulments

An annulment decree differs from a divorce decree in that it does not presuppose a marriage at all; what the parties may have believed to be a marriage was invalid because of fraud or other reasons. Therefore, although there may be support paid to a wife and children after an annulment, the usual rights and duties which accompany a valid marriage, such as inheritance and dower rights, do not have to be considered.

The varying provisions of our state laws on this subject cause problems similar to those which arise in cases of foreign (or out-of-state) divorces.

Separation

A separation action (or limited divorce) may be brought by either the husband or the wife in most of our states. This is *not* a divorce but is a legal remedy which provides for the separate maintenance of parties who no longer wish to live together as husband and wife. It must be brought by the party who was not at fault. Some of the permissible causes include: cruelty, non-support by the husband, desertion, habitual drunkenness and violent conduct. Such a suit does not hinder the complaining party from a later suit for a divorce. The separation may be revoked by the voluntary cohabitation of the parties or their joint application to the court.

Support of the innocent party and of the children is provided for by payments of alimony while the separation is in force. Some states also provide for a property division of the spouses. The rights of the spouses in each other's property after death is not affected by a separation unless they specifically agree that this be so. It is interesting to note that two states, NORTH CAROLINA and PENNSYLVANIA allow alimony in this type of divorce (called a "divorce from bed and board" in some states) while they do not allow it in absolute divorce. In NORTH CAROLINA such alimony may not exceed one third of the husband's annual income.

In a great many cases, instead of bringing suit against each other and allowing the court to determine their respective rights, couples who have separated may contract with each other as to the support of the wife and custody of the children. These SEPARATION AGREEMENTS will be upheld by courts if they are not unfair to either party or if they do not interfere with the welfare and rights of the children. They will not be upheld if there is any evidence that the wife was forced to enter into agreements by pressure from the husband or any other person. (For a sample separation agreement see Appendix E.)

Chapter II

PARENTAL SUPPORT

We can trace the "relatives' responsibility" tradition within our public assistance programs back to 1597, in Section 7, Chapter 3, 39th Elizabeth, An Act for the Relief of the Poor, which states:

> That the parents or children of every poor, old, blind, lame and impotent person, or other poor personnot able to work, being of sufficient ability, shall at their own charges relieve and maintain every such poor person in that manner and according to that rate as by the justices at their general quarter session shall be assessed.

This charge- to insure the economic support of one's parents or children- was to remain intact for more than three hundred years in both welfare statutes and civil codes in England and in the United States.

The gradual erosion of the requirement that adult children take responsibility for their aged or infirm parents began in this country with the failure of some newer states, principally those in South and West, to enact filial responsibility laws as had those in the East, which had been influenced more by the Puritan traditions. One historian has suggested that enforcement of filial responsibility eroded more quickly in this country than in did enforcement of parental responsibility because of the fact that aged parents continued to maintain ownership of their farmlands until death, when their children, who had been living with their elderly parents, became owners. The elderly were thus not economically dependent until after the rise of industrialized cities, which broke this centuries-old tradition by luring the young from their parents' rural homes. The elderly parents were then left without kin to work the farms when they became too feeble to do so, and the children grew old in the cities where few had maintained the tradition of living in extended family arrangements. Separate homesites and growing geographic separation owing to the westward movement tended to erode filial ties.

The traditions of filial responsibility which had been enunciated in the Poor Laws were incorporated in early Social Security legislation, which provided for survivors' benefits to be paid to the aged, dependent parents of a covered wage earner in the event of his or her death. The public assistance portion of the Social Security Act, which set up the adult categories including Old Age Assistancem left the question of filial responsibility up to the states. By 1952, most of the states had legislation requiring support that was clearly applicable to OAA recipients only, seven states had general legislation that did not specifically apply to OAA recipients, and twelve had no legislation at all which required support. The last vestiges of economic responsibility for aged or disabled parents was removed from their adult children by the time OAA was federalized in 1973. No longer are the children of SSI recipients subjected to a means test. This decline in public assistance regulations that were designed to foster filial responsibility has corresponded with a diminution in the proportion of the elderly who had been employed in "uncovered" occupations, as well as a decline in the proportion of the poor who were aged.

As more elderly people became eligible for Social Security benefits, fewer were to be found in poverty. Thus, there has been less necessity for enforcing filial responsibility as a means of limiting public assistance expenditures.

The responsibility of parents for the economic maintenance of their minor children has not been eroded as that of adults for their aged parents. In fact, there has been a trend in recent years to accelerate the enforcement of the parental support obligation.

As with laws requiring adult children to support their aged parents, the public is not concerned with the enforcement of child support unless the dependent person is poor. Even in states whose civil codes allow it, it is unlikely that parents with incomes lower than public assistance standards can compel support from a wealthy child, no matter how desperate their circumstances. The public enforcement of filial support laws has only been stimulated in times of sharply rising public assistance costs.

In 1950, because of congressional concern that greater efforts should be made to enforce the assumption of parental responsibility in families receiving what was then called Aid to Dependent Children, the NOLEO ("notice to law enforcement officials") amendment was added to Title IV D of the Social Security Act. In order to continue to receive federal monies for state-administered welfare programs, the states were required to "provide prompt notice to appropriate law-enforcement officials, of the furnishing of aid to dependent children in respect of a child who has been deserted or abandoned by a parent.

This represented the first time since the passage of the Social Security Act that states were *mandated* to involve themselves in the legal process for enforcing a civil code. In addition, the NOLEO marked the point at which the option for taking legal action against the father of her child was removed from a woman applying for or receiving public aid.

In an effort to facilitate enforcement of NOLEO, the Uniform Reciprocal Enforcement of Support Act (URESA) was promulgated by the National Conference on Uniform State Laws in 1950. Within a short time, all the states, plus the District of Columbia, Guam, Puerto Rico, and the Virgin Islands had made formal agreements with one another and/or enacted legislation consistent with URESA. The specific provisions preclude the possibility that movement across state lines per se will facilitate the avoidance of the obligation of a parent to support his children. Thus, the parent with custody does not have to go to the errant parent's state of residence to secure support through his court of jurisdiction, nor does the absent parent have to be extradited to the state in which the dependent children live. It was felt by policymakers that the adoption of URESA by all the states, together with the NOLEO welfare amendment of 1950, would facilitate the enforcement of support for ADC-dependent children and thereby help reduce the public outlay for this group.

That the intrusion into the previously private decisions of families should have come about in the form of the NOLEO amendments is not surprising in light of what had been happening in the AFDC population. Liberalized welfare regulations in the fourties had shortened waiting periods for establishment of "continued absence" of the father from the home and lifted restrictions that had previously excluded illegitimate children from eligibility. These, together with the increasing rates of divorce, separation, and illegitimacy, have resulted in an unexpected burgeoning of the welfare rolls.

By 1967, Congress was apparently convinced that the NOLEO requirement and the supporting legislation, URESA, were not effective enough in terms of reducing the growing AFDC costs and caseloads, for the Senate Finance Committee instituted what it believed would be an effective program of enforcement of child support and determination of paternity. It proposed Social Security amendments requiring that the state welfare agency establish a single, identified unit, whose purpose was to undertake to establish paternity of each child receiving welfare who was born out of wedlock and to secure support for him or her. This proposed legislation was adopted, and the scope of involvement in the legal and domestic affairs of the poor was thereby broadened. The state now has mandate not only to notify law enforcement officials that the civil code requiring fathers to provide support was being violated, but also to initiate and accomplish the activity of determining paternity.

Parent Locator Service

Regardless of whether a state or the custodial parent institutes proceedings for enforcement of support obligations, a major difficulty in the enforcement of support duties is locating the obligor for services of process. Although it is recognized that local locator services often operate more effectively than those organized on a state or national level, local efforts to trace deserting parents have been hampered by a lack of cooperation and aid from federal and state offices.

In the past, there were several means of obtaining

information concerning the location of an absent parent. Federal law permitted any state or local welfare agency to obtain the obligor's address or last known employer's address from the Department of Health and Welfare or the Internal Revenue Service under certain conditions. This information could also be acquired by any court having jurisdiction to issue support orders for a particular child. So while no individual could obtain the absent parent's address directly from the federal government under prior law, welfare parents could often obtain it through a Court or welfare agency, while non-welfare parents had to secure the information through a court or use private sources.

Most states provide centralized locator services having the same functions as the new federal system. Among the best known are the offices obtained in New York, California, Maine, Maryland and Connecticut. The New York Bureau of Registry and Location is typical of these programs. It maintains full records on persons who have deserted juvenile welfare recipients. Its files include the parent's name, aliases, last known address, date and place of birth, physical description, social security number, employment history, any military or police record, as well as information concerning any support proceedings instituted against him (or her) and other relevant facts derived from official or non-official sources. The Bureau only supplements locator services operated by various communities but it processes eight to nine hundred requests for information each month and statistics show that it provides "useful" information in 45.5 percent of its cases.

The new federal Parent Locator Service is designed to provide more persons with access to more information necessary to enforce support obligations. It is established within the Department of Health and Welfare and directed by an appointee of the Secretary of that department. Those authorized to use the service are: any parent, guardian or attorney acting on behalf of an abandoned child, any official of a court having jurisdiction to issue a support order in the case, and any agency of a state participating in the federal AFDC program. Non-welfare parents who need the information to institute support proceedings may use the Parent Locator Service on a fee basis.

Under the law, the Secretary of Health and Welfare has the authority to obtain the necessary data not only from the files of the Department but also "from any other department, agency, or instrumentality, of the United States or of any state." There are two prerequisites to disclosure of any information by the Secretary: first, the information must be requested for use in enforcing support obligations; and second, the person or organization making the request must have exhausted all available state and local sources of information. If the Secretary is satisfied that both these prerequisites have been met, he shall disclose the absent parent's address or his last known employer's address to aid in locating the obligor, although the information will not be released if its disclosure would violate the confidential nature of census data or infringe upon national security.

The federal locator service has clear advantages over current state systems. It provides central access to information which has been dispersed among various state and federal agencies and it removes the obstacles of expense, time, and geographical separation which have precluded use of many of these sources of information. As a result, more persons have access to more information regarding the people they are investigating.

Support and Custody

It is generally the father who is charged with the support of his minor children. There are criminal statutes in all of the states making it a misdemeanor or felony for a man to neglect his children. (These statutes are often a part of the previously mentioned laws relating to the desertion of a wife by a husband.) If the child has no father, then the person having custody over him is considered the parent, and has the same duties and obligations which a natural father would have. In some states, both parents must support the children, but this usually comes into effect only when the father is unable to do so. Support means proper physical care and a fitting education for the child according to the means of his family and his station in life.

The parents of a child or sometimes only the father, are also the natural guardians of a child. In this capacity they must look after his interests. Where the child has no father or mother, the court may appoint a guardian for him. Most states provide that a child over fourteen years of age may choose his own guardian if his choice is one approved by the court.

If the child is an illegitimate one whose father has not acknowledged him, his mother is his natural guardian and has sole custody over him.

Fathers' Liability for Necessaries

The parent is obligated to support the child until he reaches the age of majority. However, if the child is physically or mentally defective, that support is a continuing one at least until the necessity for support ceases—if it ever does. This continuing support cannot be evaded by neglect, improper contract, or any other unjustifiable means. The legal liability of a parent for his child is not even removed if that parent has gone through a bankruptcy proceeding and was discharged from all legal obligations.

There is nothing in a child's conduct which terminates the parent's support obligation. That obligation is not terminated because the child has acted rudely, disrespectfully, or disobediently toward the parent, or because the child has quit school against the parent's wishes. However, the question of emancipation may come up in these matters.

If the child lives away from home and is self-supporting, the parent is not liable for ordinary expenses. if a parent is willing to support the child in his own home and the child chooses to stay away without justifiable reasons, the parent is not liable for his support. Again, the question is made to turn on the effect of the child's absence as an emancipation. This is especially so when the question involves liability for medical services. In some states statutes expressly provide that a parent is not liable for the support of a child who has left him without just cause. But if the conduct of the parent is what drove the child away from home, or if he abandons the child, he is liable for necessaries. This is true even in the case of an adopted child.

But the person furnishing the necessaries has the burden of providing that there was an unjustified abandonment, that the support furnished was necessary, and that the credit of the father was the basis of the advances.

The father's liability for necessaries furnished his minor child is not affected by the fact that custody was awarded to the mother, unless he has also been relieved of his support duty. If there is no provision for either custody or support and the children live with the mother, the father is liable to her and to third persons who provide necessaries. It is not defense to the third person's claim against the father that his liability, as between parents, is limited by the support provisions of a divorce decree. On the other hand, if the mother leaves the father without his assent, or without proper justification, taking their children with her, the father is usually not held liable for necessaries later furnished to the children by the mother or by a third person. Some courts do not follow this rule on the ground that the misconduct of the mother should not prejudice the rights of the children. This is especially persuasive where the father has made no effort to regain the custody of the children. Of course, if the father has been guilty of neglect or cruelty so that the mother was essentially obliged to leave him, he continues to be liable for necessaries furnished to the children. And the father's liability also continues where the mother, living apart, has custody of the children by mutual consent or agreement.

Persons in Loco Parentis

If a person puts himself in the situation of a lawful parent by assuming the obligations incident to the parental relation without going through the formalities necessary to a legal adoption, he is said to stand *in loco parentis*. Guardians also stand *in loco parentis* and may be held liable to the child for failure to carry out the duties imposed on them in this connection.

This relationship of *in loco parentis* is established only when the person intends to assume the status of a parent toward the child. Perhaps the clearest evidence of consent to stand *in loco parentis* is when a person takes a child not his own into his custody as a member of his own family. But *intent* must be proved.

Once it is established that one stands in loco parentis to another, the rights and liabilities arising out of that relation are substantially the same as being a legal or blood-related parent.

Child Support of Parents

In a number of states there are statutes imposing on children, to the extent of their ability, the duty to support indigent parents. These statutes, aimed at relieving the state or local authorities from the burden of supporting poor persons who have relatives able to care for them, are usually treated as a part of the "poor" laws of the state, enforceable in some states by criminal proceedings. Statutes sometimes make adult children liable for maintenance of a parent in a state institution.

Illegitimate Children

An illegitimate child, according to the law, means "a person begotten and born out of lawful wedlock."

The definition is a very clear one where there has been no marriage at all between the parties but it must be remembered that there are a number of marriages which are declared void at a later date. There are statutory provisions making the children of a marriage which has been dissolved legitimate. However, the legitimacy of the children of a void marriage is sometimes dependent upon the circumstances of the marriage and the good faith of one or both partners. If both parties, realizing their lack of capacity to contract a valid marriage, nevertheless attempt to do so, the children may be declared illegitimate. The children of an incestuous or of a mixed race marriage are usually illegitimate by a statute in those states prohibiting such marriages.

Where there has been a valid marriage there is a strong legal presumption that the children of the marriage are legitimate. This presumption is based upon principles of natural justice. Unless the husband is proven to have been absent for a certain length of time during the period when conception occurs, the wife's children are deemed by the law to be his own. Even in those cases where there is evidence of the wife's adultery and a consequent divorce, there must be additional proof to render her children illegitimate. Where it is obvious that conception has taken place before marriage, the child is nevertheless presumed to be the child of the husband and wife.

The children who are illegitimate because their parents have never married present a serious problem as to their support and care. At common law such a child was a "son of nobody" and neither parent could be held responsible for it. The original laws imposing support of the child on a parent were enacted solely to prevent the community from having the child as a public charge.

It is this concern over added public burdens rather than a social conscience which has made it possible in a number of states for the state's attorney, or the public welfare authorities, to bring an action against the man who is accused of being the father of the child. If the mother of the child cannot afford her own attorney, she has recourse to such a procedure.

Whether the action is brought by the state's attorney or by the mother of the child, the court procedure is essentially the same. The reputed father is brought into court by a summons or by a warrant of arrest, depending upon whether the law of the state makes the action a civil or a criminal one. There is usually a preliminary hearing before a justice of the peace, county judge, or similar officer. There may then be a trial by jury. The accused is required to give a bond as security pending the actual determination of paternity only if the judge has reason to believe that the man is the father of the child. Such actions may be brought in the county where the child was born or where the father resides. They must be brought within a certain time, usually two years, after the birth of the child.

After a man has been adjudged to be the father of an

illegitimate child, he is usually expected to assist with its support and to pay the expenses of the mother's confinement. The amount of support varies according to the state statutes. There are a few states which impose upon the father, or upon both parents, the same obligations as they would have if the child were a legitimate one. Among these are ARIZONA, MINNESOTA, NEBRASKA, NEW JERSEY and NORTH CAROLINA. The ARIZONA statute is remarkable because it completely does away with the distinction made between legitimate and illegitimate, stating as follows:

> "Every child is the legitimate child of its natural parents and is entitled to support and education as if born in lawful wedlock, except the right to dwelling or a residence with the family of its father if such father be married. It shall inherit from its natural parents and from their kindred heir, lineal and collateral, in the same manner as children born in lawful wedlock. This section shall apply to cases where the natural father of any such child is married to one other than the mother of said child, as well as when he is single."

NEBRASKA imposes liability for support upon the mother of the child only when it is not practical to secure support from the father. The statute in that state, as is true of a few other states, expressly provides for an illegitimate child to be called a "child born out of wedlock" in all proceedings instead of by the usual term "bastard."

In most other states the court determines the amount of support which the father must pay. Generally the mother has the chief burden of support even though he is legally bound to assist her. Some of the states even limit the amounts which a father can be required by the court to pay, and a brief glance at these sums will show that their chief characteristic is their *striking inadequacy*.

FLORIDA: Not more than $50.00 per year for ten years, in addition to the necessary expenses of birth.

ILLINOIS: Not more than $200.00 for the first year, not more than $100.00 per year for the next nine years.

OREGON: $100.00 to $350.00 per year for the first two years $150.00 to $500.00 per year for the next twelve years.

SOUTH CAROLINA: Approximately $30.00 to $100.00 per year for twelve years.

TENNESSEE: Not more than $60.00 per year for twelve years, only if the child is likely to become a public charge.

UTAH: Not more than $200.00 for the first year, not more than $150.00 per year for the next seventeen years.

The father, when determined by law to be such, may be required to give a bond as a guarantee for the support which the court has ordered. In a number of states the mother must disclose the father but if she refuses to do so, she herself must then furnish a bond, especially if it is likely that the child will become a public burden. A number of states provide that the father's estate is liable for a child's support if he dies before it becomes of age.

These proceedings are usually permitted to single women only, because of the rule of evidence that married couples cannot give testimony in court which would make their children bastards. However, in some cases a married woman whose husband is known to be absent may bring an action against the father of her child to obtain support from him. In WEST VIRGINIA, for example, the proceedings may be brought by a married woman against a putative father if she has not been living with her husband for one year previous to the action.

In addition to the difficulties of proving a man to be the father of a child (most women are reluctant to make a public attempt to obtain the necessary support for their children) there is the additional problem of enforcement. If the man is in the same county or state as the mother the threat of a jail sentence may force him to make the payments ordered, but what of the man who leaves the state?

The deserting father is the same problem to his family and to the community as the deserting husband. To meet this problem seven states, IOWA, NEW MEXICO, NEW YORK, NEVADA, NORTH and SOUTH DAKOTA and WYOMING have enacted a Uniform Legitimacy Act. One purpose of this act is to enable a mother to proceed by law against the father of her child even though he has gone to another state. Where there has been a judgment by a court against the man in one state for the support of his child, this judgment may be made a domestic judgment in another state and be sued upon where the father now resides. It is not necessary for the mother of an illegitimate child to be a resident of the state in order to bring proceedings against the father compelling him to support it.

Other provisions of the uniform laws attempt to protect the child as much as possible. *Both* of his parents are obligated to give him support and education until he reaches the age of sixteen. When the defendant father has died, an action for support may be brought against his personal representatives. Where there has been an agreement or compromise between the mother and the accused father, this agreement will be binding on the mother and child *only* where the court decides that it is an adequate agreement. If the father defaults, without excuse, to support a child of which he has been adjudged the father or which he has acknowledged in writing, he is subject to a criminal liability and may pay a fine of $1000 or serve a year in prison, or both.

The support of the illegitimate child is another illustration of the divergence between the law and its enforcement. Social studies, such as those of Ruth Reed,[2] show that not only is there a reluctance on the part of the deserted mother to refer to the child's father, but there is a strong tendency on the part of most of these fathers to disappear. Most women are not in a financial position to search for such a man, and therefore the burden of the child's care is most often thrust upon others, either relatives or social agencies.

There are few complete records of the support actually given to these children by their legally proven fathers. Dr. Reed estimated that the total collection of the Department

---

[2] Reed, Ruth: *The Illegitimate Family in New York City*, published for the Welfare Council of New York City, Columbia University Press, 1934.

of Welfare in New York City in its Filiation Proceedings would amount to approximately $50.00 per child per year. However, since the Department had not reported the number of its open cases, the amount cannot be more than an estimate. Nevertheless, most studies indicate that the support of the child by the father is negligible when compared with its total needs. It is not the purpose of this small book to suggest legislative and social improvements. Suffice it to say that, in this particular field as well as in other fields of support, there is much room for improvement.

The inheritance rights of an illegitimate child are usually limited, even when his father has been determined. As a general rule the child is considered to be the child of the mother only, and inherits from her. Rarely does the law give illegitimate children the same rights as legitimate ones; NEW HAMPSHIRE is one of the few states in which the mother's estate descends equally to her legitimate and illegitimate offspring. Acknowledgment of the child by the father in writing or by public announcement makes the child the heir of the father also, although it cannot inherit from the father's kindred unless the parents have married each other. Such marriage. and subsequent recognition or adoption, changes the child's status.

In some states the right of an illegitimate child to take under a Will is limited when there are also legitimate children. The words "heirs," "children," and "issue" do not usually mean illegitimate children; therefore if the testator intends to include them among his beneficiaries he should be specific about it.

Adoption

The legal procedure necessary for the adoption of a child or of an adult varies from state to state and is discussed in a previous volume of this series. Since the legal effect of an adoption is, generally, the severance of the parent and child relation of the child with its natural parents, one may rightly assume that the natural parents have no further obligation to support the child after the adoption is completed. This is true in the majority of cases, but there may be exceptions. There is an ILLINOIS case which holds that the natural parents may, if the necessity exists, still have a duty to support a child which has been adopted by others. For purposes of support, the adopted child is in the same position as if it were the natural child of the adopting parents. The obligation is a reciprocal one, so that the child also has a duty toward its new parents and must support them when he becomes of age if they are in need.

For purposes of inheritance, the state laws vary. In the majority of states, no distinction is made between a natural child and a child by adoption. In these cases, the child shall inherit from its adoptive parents and they shall inherit from him. There are a number of variations in the inheritance laws of the states. Some laws permit a child to inherit from the adoptive parents but not from their kindred as he would inherit if he were a natural child, that is, he is not on a par with the brothers and sisters which he acquired by reason of his adoption. Others state that property which is limited to "heirs of the body" of the adopters does not descend to the adopted child. If a Will or a deed of trust is worded in this manner it does not include children who are adopted. NEW JERSEY, OKLAHOMA, RHODE ISLAND, VERMONT and WEST VIRGINIA have this provision in their laws.

The rights of the adoptive parents are also limited by some states. In GEORGIA the petitioner who adopted the child may never inherit from him. ILLINOIS permits the adopting parents to take from a deceased adopted child only such property as he had received from or through them. OKLAHOMA and VIRGINIA exclude property that has come to the child through his blood kindred from the inheritance rights of his adopters.

A child who has been adopted is usually denied the right to inherit from his natural parents since he is no longer considered to be legally related to them. However, some states specifically provide that he may inherit from them.

This right is included in the adoption statutes of FLORIDA, KENTUCKY, MAINE and NEW YORK. As a general rule, the natural parents do not have the reciprocal rights to inherit from a child which has been adopted.

There are other qualifications on the inheritance of both parents and child in some states. LOUISIANA makes the adopted child the same as a natural child in all respects except that the adoption shall never interfere with the rights of "forced" heirs.[3] MISSISSIPPI has no limiting statute but provides that the petition of adoption must state all of the benefits that are to be conferred upon the person to be adopted.

Since there is a legal procedure necessary in most states preliminary to an adoption, the respective rights of the parties may be ascertained at the time of the adoption. In a few states an illegitimate child becomes legitimate and adopted when his father publicly acknowledges him and takes him into his home, without any legal proceeding.

---

[3] Certain relatives are given preference over others.

Chapter III

PUBLIC SUPPORT

Support of Paupers

In most of our states certain relatives are responsible for the support of a pauper. Appendix F shows the relatives liable in each state. Liability may be divided between close relatives, or the state or county may determine those best able to assist with his maintenance. In a few states, liability is determined by relationship, that is, the parents or children are primarily liable, but if they are unable or absent, less close relatives may be called upon.

Where there are liable relatives, the state or county may sue such relatives for his maintenance if the pauper has become a public charge. The amounts payable to the government vary.

In those states where the relatives are not legally responsible, the local or state authorities assume this responsibility by means of taxation for the purpose.

A few states, such as MINNESOTA and ILLINOIS, limit the liability of relations to parents and children when the pauper has become poor because of his own intemperance or bad conduct.

These statutes imposing liability on relatives have of course nothing to do with a man's obligation to his wife and children. These, as has been mentioned, are found in all states.

Workmens Compensation Laws

The Workmen's Compensation Acts were enacted in the States in order to insure certain employees against the natural hazards of their employment. These are state laws and now exist in each of the United States. They are fairly recent in origin and are a result of the development of the social and economic idea that the cost of such accidents shall fall on those most able to bear it, that is, the employers or their insurers rather than on the employees. Formerly, and at common law, the only recourse an injured workman had was to bring an action at law for damages against his employer. Since the employer in these actions had as a defense the possible negligence of the employee and his assumption of risk when he undertook that type of employment, recovery by workmen was uncertain.

These acts provide for insurance in specified types of employment. Insurance may be effected through a private company, by means of a state fund, or by the self-insurance of the employer. In the latter case the employer must prove to the satisfaction of the compensation board of his state that he is financially able to pay compulsory claims. Compensation insurance is compulsory in some states and elective in others. Compulsory insurance may exist with respect to certain occupations. Election to come under the state act is presumed in some states where the employer has not openly rejected to do so.

Not all kinds of employment are covered. The state laws vary in this particular. Coverage may be determined by the nature of the employment and sometimes by the number of employees engaged by one employer or company. The most common distinction made by state laws is that between hazardous and non-hazardous occupations. The law may be compulsory as to the former and elective by the employer as to the latter. In some states hazardous occupations are listed as such by the applicable statutes and in others the court decisions are the determining factor in classification. Employment for a limited period of time, casual employment, is generally not covered, nor is that by volunteer workers, although a contract of hire might make a volunteer a regular worker.

Certain groups of workers are generally excluded also, namely, persons engaged in agriculture or domestic service. Professional workers as those in law and medicine, do not usually come under state compensation laws. An independent contractor who is hired to do a certain piece of work, such as a plumber or a roofer, may not claim compensation if he is injured while on the job. The test in these cases is the measure of control the workman has over the manner of doing the work.

Two factors must be present for an injury to be compensable. It must have resulted from an accident and must have occurred during the course of the worker's regular employment. Brief reflection on these two qualifications will show that both of these may not always be clearly definable. Courts define an accident as "a result produced by a fortuitous cause" or "an unexpected or unforeseen event, happening suddenly and violently, with or without human fault." There must be a linking cause between the accident and the resultant injury. There are numerous instances where a slight additional strain has caused bodily damage, such as a rupture or a heart attack. Some of the courts give a liberal interpretation to the word "accident" and go so far as to consider the injury itself to be the accident.

"In the course of employment" usually means having to do with and originating in the work or affairs which are necessarily incident to it. There may be times when there will be much controversy as to this factor, such as when an employee collapses after he reaches home because of excessive heat while he was at work or because of extra exertion. Accidents during lunch hour are not usually compensable, but a number of decisions now permit recovery for injuries during "horseplay" between employees while they are at work, holding that such play is a natural result of a group of men at work together. When an injury occurs during a rest period, compensation is allowable in some states, since the workman was doing what he might have reasonably been expected to do at that time. Likewise, an employee injured on the premises before and after working hours is usually allowed compensation. Traveling in course of the employer's business constitutes employment.

Compensation laws, however, cover not only industrial accidents, but also "occupational diseases." There are provisions for compensation for occupational diseases in all of the states with the exception of ALABAMA, IOWA, KANSAS, LOUISIANA, NEVADA, NEW HAMPSHIRE, OKLAHOMA, SOUTH CAROLINA, SOUTH DAKOTA, TENNESSEE, TEXAS, VERMONT, and WYOMING. An occupational disease is one which usually develops gradually from the effects of long continued work at a kind of employment known to have this risk incident to it. The most common occupational diseases are silicosis, a lung disease resulting from the inhalation of dust, and those connected with poisoning by industrial products. The state statutes may list these diseases in a schedule or provide for coverage by broader definitions. Since these diseases are still an inevitable result of most present working conditions in the employments which cause them, coverage by compensation laws is most important for a worker engaged in certain industries.

Employees not covered by state compensation acts may come under other laws, such as the Federal Compensation Act for civil employees of the United States, the Longshoremen's Act for stevedores and the Federal Employer's Liability Act for those engaged in interstate commerce, such as railroading.

Just what compensation is an injured worker entitled to? This depends upon the nature of the injury, the employee's wage at the time and, if he is killed, the number and relation of his dependents. All injuries may be grouped under the following headings:

Temporary partial disability
Permanent partial disability
Temporary total disability
Permanent total disability

Death
Medical expenses
Funeral expenses

The injured man or woman does not receive the former total wages as compensation but only a percentage thereof, from 50 to 66 2/3 percent of the weekly amount earned. This is received for a definite number of weeks. Death benefits are paid to widows or children.

All employed persons should ascertain at once whether they are covered by the Act of their state, and also the proper authority to notify in the case of an injury. The state laws require notice to the employer within a limited period of time, and the filing of a claim with the administrative authorities. Compensation cases are heard informally before a board, but a decision is always appealable to the proper court. An employee never needs the assistance of an attorney at the hearing of his case.

Social Security - Historical Background

In 1889, nearly 50 years beofre the U.S. Social Security Act, Otto von Bismark, the Iron Chancellor of Germany, established the first social security system providing old-age pensions. This bold step called for compulsory participation of workers in a plan for old-age insurance supported by contributions from workers and employers, with benefits related to earnings levels. Austria followed Germany in 1906 with a compulsory social insurance plan, and Romania in 1912. In England the development of social security had its roots in voluntary associations and friendly societies begun in the early 1860s. A noncontributory, income-tested government pension system was established in 1908, followed in 1925 by a contributory plan of flat benefits that contrasted with the German and other systems of wage-related benefits. By 1926 all of the European state had established contributory old-age insurance plans. In 1933 it was commented by one writer that "China, India, and the United States are the only large countries still remaining without any national system of old age security."

At the 1917 national convention of the Progressive Party Theodore Roosevelt urged that "we must protect the crushable elements at the base of our present industrial structure ... It is abnormal for any industry to throw back upon the community the human wreckage due to its wear and tear." He called for a response to "the hazards of sickness, accident, invalidism, involuntary unemployment, and old age" by providing insurance. In spite of these sensitive remarks by one of America's great individualists, many Americans tended to look upon adversities such as unemployment and poverty in old age as weaknesses of individuals and not of the economy or of the society. Nor did the contrary voices of Eugene V. Debs and Norman Thomas attract many followers. Not until the cataclysm of the Great Depression did Americans generally conclude that forces stronger than the individual were at work and that other nations had advanced beyond the United States in social programs.

It was a deep depression which by late 1932 had resulted in a creeping bank paralysis across the nation. And by 1933 unemployment had risen to an unprecedented 13 million pensions, nearly one out of every five in the civilian work force. Many of the Federal Government's measures to meet the crisis of the depression were necessarily temporary, but President Franklin D. Roosevelt came to realize that many aspects of the crisis were symptoms of a need for greater attention to underlying social and economic forces. In his message to Congress of June 8, 1934, he stressed the need for more than temporary measures, emphasizing decent housing, productive work, and "some safeguards against the misfortunes which cannot be wholly eliminated in this man-made world of ours."

To develop proposals and make recommendations for the implementation of long-range measures of economic security, the President established by Executive Order (June 29, 1934) a Committee on Economic Security composed of Frances Perkins, Henry Morganthau, Henry A. Wallace, Homer Cummings, and Harry Hopkins (respectively, Secretaries of Labor, Treasury, and Agriculture, Attorney General, and Federal Emergency Relief Administrator).

As discussion of the proposed program developed, Roosevelt took special pains to assure the country that the new plan was a sound program started on a reasonable scale. The work of the planning and technical committees led to a final report to the President, dated January 5, 1935. This report contained the recommendations leading to landmark legislation later in the year, the Social Security Act, passed and signed August 14, 1935.

This 1935 act was put together quickly by the "brain trust" and college professors. It soon appeared that the benefits would have to be improved and the methods of determining benefit amounts and insured status changed. There was time for alterations to be made, since the original act had provided for taxes to begin in 1937 and benefits in 1942. The changes were incorporated in the Social Security Amendments of 1939, which substantially recast the whole program, added survivors' benefits, and advanced the starting date for monthly benefits from 1942 to 1940.

During World War II and its aftermath, practically no change was made in the infant social security program other than to postpone payroll tax increases. But the low benefit levels of the program came increasingly under criticism.

The year 1950 began a period of new growth for the Social Security system, gradual at first, then accelerating. Amendments in 1950 brought under coverage the nonagricultural self-employed and Americans employed outside the United States by American employers. Workers in Puerto Rico and the Virgin Islands were added. Coverage of state and local government employees not under a retirement system was made elective by the employer, and coverage of employees of nonprofit organizations was made elective by employer and employee. Changes in 1954 made it possible for state and local government employees belonging to a state retirement system to be covered by election of employer and employees, and brought in self-employed farm workers and professional people. The armed forces, along with additional professional people, were covered by changes made in 1956. Total disability benefits were added for workers aged 50 and over by 1954. Four years later the disability coverage was extended to all covered workers regardless of age. Medicare for persons 65 and older was added in 1965 and long-term (two years or more) disabled beneficiaries in 1972. Benefit levels were raised 10 different times between 1950 and 1972. By far the largest benefit changes made in the Social Security program were voted by Congress in 1972 to become effective in 1973 and later. And in following years even greater benefits have been established in an attempt to keep up with the inflationary spiral of the late 1970s.

Building Protection

Before you or your family can get monthly cash benefits, you must have credit for a certain amount of work under social security. The exact amount of work credit depends on your age.

Social security credit is measured in "quarters of coverage." Starting with 1978, employees and self-employed people receive one quarter of coverage for each $250 of covered annual earnings. No more than four quarters of coverage can be credited for a year. The $250 measure will increase automatically in the future to keep pace with average wages.

Before 1978, an employee generally earned one quarter of coverage if he or she was paid wages of $50 or more in a calendar quarter. Self-employed people received four quarters of coverage if they had a self-employment net profit of $400 or more.

If you stop working under social security before you have earned enough credit, you cannot get benefits later. But the credit you have already earned will stay on your record and you can add to it if you return to work under social security.

Having enough credit means only that you or your family can get checks. The amount of your check depends on your average earnings over a period of years.

Amount of Monthly Checks

Up to now, social security checks have usually been based

on your average earnings under social security over a period of years, using the actual dollar value of your past earnings. This method will continue to be used for workers who reach 62, become disabled, or die before 1979.

For workers who reach 62, become disabled, or die after 1978 a new method of calculating benefits will got into effect. Under this method, actual earnings for past years will be adjusted to take account of changes in average wages since 1951. These adjusted earnings will be averaged together and a formula will be applied to the average to determine the benefit amount.

The new method is intended to insure that benefits will reflect changes in wage levels over your working lifetime and will have a relatively constant relationship to pre-retirement earnings. So that no one now nearing retirement will be disadvantaged, the law contains a guarantee. Under the guarantee, retirement benefits for workers who reach 62 after 1978 and before 1984 will be figured two ways—under the old method using benefit rates that were in effect as of January 1979 and under the new method. The benefit rate paid will be the higher of the two calculations.

In addition, social security benefits for people on the rolls will increase automatically in future years as the cost of living rises. Each year, living costs will be compared with those of the year before. If living costs have increased 3 percent or more, benefits will be increased by the same amount and will be included in checks issued the following July unless Congress have already acted to increase benefits.

While you are working, social security contributions are taken out of your wages. You will pay social security contributions on all wages up to $17,700 in 1978. After increases to $22,900 in 1980, and $29,700 in 1981, this amount will increase automatically in future years to keep up with changes in average wage levels as under previous law. This means that a worker paying increased social security contributions can be sure of higher benefits later because benefits will be based on a higher level of earnings.

Social security checks are not subject to Federal income tax.

If you qualify for checks on the record of more than one worker (for example, on your own record and your husband's or wife's), you will receive an amount equal to the larger of the two amounts. If, in addition to your social security benefit as a wife, husband, or widower, you receive a pension based on your work in public employment not covered by social security, your benefit as a dependent or survivor will be reduced by the amount of that pension. Under an exception in the law, your governmental pension will not affect your dependent's or survivor's benefit if you become eligible for that pension before December 1982, and, if at the time you apply or become entitled to your social security benefit as a dependent or survivor, you could have qualified for that benefit if the law as in effect January 1977 had remained in effect. (At that time, men had to prove they were dependent upon their wives for their support to be eligible for benefits as a dependent or survivor.) Your government pension, however, will not affect any social security benefit based on your own work covered by social security.

In addition to monthly payments, there is a lump-sum payment made at a worker's death. It is $255.

A Word of Explanation

Some people think that if they have always earned the maximum amount covered by social security they will get the highest benefit shown on the chart. This is not so. Although retirement benefits as high as $502 a month are shown, payments this high cannot be paid to a worker retiring at 65 now. The maximum retirement benefit generally payable to a worker who becomes 65 in 1978 is $489.70 a month (effective June 1978) based on average yearly earnings of $8,257.

The reason the average can be no higher now is that the maximum covered earnings were lower in past years. Those years of lower limits must be counted in with the higher ones of recent years to figure your average covered yearly earnings and this average determines the amount of your check.

The maximum earnings creditable for social security are $3,600 for 1951-1954; $4200 for 1955-1958; $4,800 for 1959-

1965; $6,600 for 1966-1967; $7,800 for 1968-1971; $9,000 for 1972; $10,800 for 1973; $13,200 for 1974; $14,100 for 1975; $15,300 for 1976; $16,500 for 1977; $17,700 for 1978; $22,900 for 1979; $25,900 for 1980; and $29,700 for 1981.

You can retire as early as 62, but your retirement check will be reduced permanently. Payment amounts are also reduced if a wife, husband, widow, or widower starts getting payments before 65.

The amount of reduction depends on the number of months you get checks before you reach 65. If you start your checks early, you will receive about the same value in total benefits over the years, but in smaller installments to take account of the longer period you will receive them.

Estimating Your Check

Although the *exact* amount of your retirement check cannot be figured until you apply for benefits, you can estimate the amount ahead of time. Ask at any social security office for a copy of the leaflet, "Estimating Your Social Security Retirement Check."

Larger Checks by Additional Work

If you return to work after you start receiving retirement checks, your added earnings will often result in higher benefits when you again stop working. Social security will automatically refigure your benefit after the additional earnings are credited to your record.

In addition, a worker who does not receive any benefits before 65 and delays retirement past 65 will get a special credit that can mean a larger benefit. The credit adds to a worker's benefit 1 percent for each year (1/12 of 1 percent for each month) from age 65 to age 72 for which he or she did not receive benefits because of work. The credit will be increased to 3 percent for each year (1/4 percent for each month) for workers reaching 65 after 1981. Also, persons who receive reduced benefits will be able to get the credit for non-payment months after reaching 65. Starting with June 1978, the worker's credit will also apply to widow's and widower's benefits.

Special Minimum Benefit

There is a special minimum benefit at retirement for some people who worked under social security over 20 years. This helps people who had low earnings (but still above a specified level) in their working years. The amount of the special minimum depends on the number of years of coverage. For a worker retiring before 1979 at 65 with 30 years of coverage, the special minimum is $180. Effective January, 1979, the special minimum for a worker with 30 or more years of coverage will increase to $230. Most people who have worked 20 years or more under social security already receive benefits higher than the special minimum.

Years of coverage from 1937 to 1950 are determined by dividing the total wages for those years by $900, with a maximum of 14 years of coverage counted for that period. After 1950, a year of coverage is any year a person has earnings of at least 25 percent of the maximum covered by social security.

The automatic cost-of-living benefit increases apply to the special minimum benefits starting in 1979.

If You Work After Payments Stop

After you start receiving social security checks, they will continue to arrive each month unless your circumstances change and cause payments to stop.

If you go back to work and are under 72, your earnings may affect your social security benefits. You do not have to stop working completely, though, to obtain social security benefits. You can receive all benefits if your earnings do not exceed the annual exempt amount. The annual amount for 1978 is $4,000 for people 65 or over and $3,240 for people under 65.

If your earnings go over the annual amount, $1 in benefits for each $2 of earnings above the limit are withheld.

The monthly measure used for 1977 and earlier years to

determine whether benefits could be paid for any month a person earned one-twelfth or less of the annual exempt amount and did not substantial work in his or her business has been eliminated. A person can use the monthly test only in the first year he or she has a month in which earnings do not exceed one-twelfth of the annual amount or does not perform substantial services in self-employment. If such a month occurs, a benefit could be paid for any month in which you earn $334 or less (if 65 or older) or $270 (if under 65) and you don't perform substantial services in self-employment even though your total yearly earnings exceed the annual amount. For people 65 or over, the annual exempt amount will increase to $4,500 for 1979; to $5,000 in 1980; $5,500 for 1981; and $6,000 for 1982. After that, the limit will increase automatically as the level of average wages rises. The limit for people under 65 will also continue to increase.

If you are receiving retirement checks, your earnings may affect your dependant's checks as well as your own. If you receive checks as a dependent or survivor, your earnings can affect only your own check.

Income That Counts

When figuring what income may affect your social security checks, you must count earnings from work of any kind, whether or not it is covered by social security, except tips amounting to less than $20 in a month with one employer. Total wages, not just take-home pay, and all net self-employment earnings must be added together.

However, income from savings, investments, or insurance will not affect your checks.

Your earnings for the entire year in which your checks start or stop count when the amount of benefits that can be paid for that year are figured. But earnings after you reach 72 won't affect your checks. Starting with 1982, earnings after you reach 70 won't affect your check.

If You Go Outside the United States

Special rules apply to people outside the United States. If you go outside the country for 30 days or more while you are receiving checks, your absence from the country may affect your right to checks. Ask at any social security office for a copy of the leaflet, "You Social Security Check While You're Outside the United States."

Financing The Basic Idea

The basic idea of social security is a simple one: During working years, employees, their employers, and self-employed people pay social security contributions. This money is used only to pay benefits to the more than 33 million people getting benefits and to pay administrative costs of the program. Then, when today's workers' earnings stop or are reduced because of retirement, death, or disability, benefits will be paid to them from contributions by people in covered employment and self-employment at that time. These benefits are intended to replace part of the earnings the family has lost.

Part of the contributions made goes for hospital insurance under Medicare so workers and their dependents will have help in paying their hospital bills when they become eligible for Medicare. The medical insurance part of Medicare is financed by premiums paid by the people who have enrolled for this protection and amounts contributed by the Federal Government.

Financing: Contribution Rates

If you are employed, you and your employer each pay an equal share of social security contributions. If you are self-employed, you pay contributions for retirement, survivors, and disability insurance at a rate about equal to one and one-half time the employee rate. The hospital insurance rate is the same for the employer, the employee, and the self-employed person.

As long as you have earnings that are covered by the law,

you continue to pay contributions regardless of your age and even if you are receiving social security benefits.

In 1979 and 1980 the employee and employer will each pay 6.13 percent. The rate for each will go to 6.65 percent in 1981; to 6.70 percent in 1982; to 7.05 percent in 1985; to 7.15 percent in 1986; and 7.65 percent in 1990.

The self-employed rate will go to 9.30 percent in 1981; to 9.35 percent in 1982; to 9.90 percent in 1985; to 10 percent in 1986; and to 10.75 percent in 1990.

The hospital insurance part of the rate will increase to 1.05 percent in 1979; 1.30 percent in 1981; 1.35 percent in 1985; and to 1.45 percent in 1986.

Funds not required for current benefit payments and expenses are invested in interest-bearing U.S. Government securities.

The Government's share of the cost for supplemental medical insurance and certain other social security costs comes from general revenues of the United States Treasury, not from social security contributions.

Financing: How Contributions Are Paid

If you are employed, your contribution is deducted from your wages each payday. Your employer matches your payment and sends the combined amount to the Internal Revenue Service.

If you are self-employed and your net earnings are more than $400 a year, you must report your earnings and pay your self-employment contribution each year when you file your individual income tax return. This is true even if you owne no income tax.

Your wages and self-employment income are entered on

your social security record throughout your working years. This record of your earnings will be used to determine your eligibility for benefits and the amount of cash benefits you and your dependents will receive.

Financing: Future Increases are Automatic

The maximum amount of annual earnings that counts for social security is $22,900 for 1979. It will rise to $25,900 for 1980; and to $29,700 for 1981. After 1981, the maximum will rise automatically in future years as earnings levels rise as it did before 1979. This will mean higher benefits later because a greater portion of a worker's earnings will be counted towards social security. Every year the increase in average covered wages will be determined, and if wage levels have increased since the base was set last, the base will be raised—but only if there is an automatic benefit increase the same year.

Financing: Excess Earnings, Contributions

When you work for more than one employer in a year and pay social security contributions on wages over the maximum amount of annual earnings that counts for social security in that year, you may claim a refund of the excess contributions on your income tax return for that year. If you work for only one employer who deducts too much in contributions, you should apply to the employer for a refund. A refund is made only when more than the required amount of contributions has been paid. Questions about contributions or refunds should be directed to the Internal Revenue Service.

Earnings over the maximum may appear on your social security earnings record, but they cannot be used to figure your benefit rate.

When You Apply for Social Security Benefits

When you apply for social security benefits, you should have with you:

1. Your own social security card or a record of your number (if your claim is on another person's record, you will need that person's card or record of the number.

2. Proof of your age; a birth certificate or a baptismal certificate made at or shortly after birth if you have one.
3. Your marriage certificate if you are applying for wife's or widow's benefits.
4. Your Form W-2 for the previous year; a copy of your last Federal income tax return if you are self-employed.

Right of Appeal

If you feel that a decision made on your claim is not correct, you may ask the Social Security Administration to reconsider it. If, after this reconsideration, you still disagree with the decision, you may ask for a hearing by an administrative law judge of the Bureau of Hearings and Appeals. And, if you are not satisfied with the hearing decision, you may request a review by the Appeals Council. If you are still not satisfied, you may take your case to the Federal Courts.

The Social Security Administration makes no charge for any of the appeals before the administration. You may, however, choose to be represented by a person of your own choice, and he or she may charge you a fee. The amount of such a fee is limited and must be approved by the Social Security Administration.

Someone in any social security office will explain how you may appeal and will help you get your claim reconsidered or request a hearing.

Supplementary Security Income

In addition to the general retirement benefit income discussed so far in this chapter, there is a Federal program called Supplemental Security Income (SSI). This program pays monthly checks to people in financial need who are 65 or older and to people in need at any age who are blind or disabled.

The aim of the program is to provide monthly checks when they are needed so that anyone who is 65 or older or blind or disabled can have a basic cash income—for one person, $177.80 a month and for a married couple $266.70.

This does not mean that every eligible person that must in his or her SSI check every month. Some people get less because they already have other income. Some get more because they live in a State that adds money to the Federal payment. In most States, a person who is eligible for SSI is also eligible for Medicaid and social services provided by the State.

People who have little or no regular cash income and who do not own much in the way of property or other things that can be turned into cash, such as stocks, bonds, jewelry, or other valuables may qualify for SSI.

A person who is single (or married but not living with his or her spouse) can have assets up to $1,500 and still receive checks. The amount for a couple is $2,250. Assets include savings accounts, stocks, bonds, jewelry, and other valuables a person or couple own.

Not everything owned counts as an asset. A home does not count. And the Federal Government does not ask for liens on the homes of people who receive SSI.

Personal affects or household goods also do not count as assets in most cases. Insurance policies or a car may not affect eligibility either, depending on their value.

People can have some money coming in and still receive SSI. The first $20 a month in income generally is not counted. Income above the first $20 a month (apart from earnings) generally reduces the amount of the SSI check. This includes social security checks, veterans compensation, worker's compensation, pensions, annuities, gifts, and other income.

For eligible people who live in someone else's household—a son's or daughter's home, for example—the SSI check may be reduced.

Supplemental Security Income is not the same as social security, even though the program is run by the Social Security Administration. But people who receive social security checks can receive SSI checks, too, if they are eligible for both. But, a person does not have to be eligible for social security to receive SSI.

If you think you may be eligible for SSI you can apply, or get more information, by contacting any social security office.

Table I
SOCIAL SECURITY BENEFITS DATA

Monthly retirement benefits (payable starting July 1978)

	For Workers				For Dependents[1]				
Average yearly earnings	Retirement at 65	at 64	at 63	at 62	Spouse at 65 or child	at 64	at 63	at 62	Family[2] benefits
$923 or less	121.80	113.70	105.60	97.50	60.90	55.90	50.80	45.70	182.70
1,200	156.70	146.30	135.90	125.40	78.40	71.90	65.40	58.80	235.10
2,600	230.10	214.80	199.50	184.10	115.10	105.50	95.90	86.40	345.20
3,000	251.80	235.10	218.30	201.50	125.90	115.40	104.90	94.50	384.90
3,400	270.00	252.00	234.00	216.00	135.00	123.80	112.50	101.30	434.90
4,000	296.20	276.50	256.80	237.00	148.10	135.70	123.40	111.10	506.20
4,400	317.30	296.20	275.00	253.90	158.70	145.40	132.20	119.10	562.50
4,800	336.00	313.60	291.20	268.80	168.00	153.90	140.00	126.00	612.70
5,200	353.20	329.70	306.20	282.60	176.60	161.80	147.20	132.50	662.70
5,600	370.60	345.90	321.20	296.50	185.30	169.80	154.40	139.00	687.10
6,000	388.20	362.40	336.50	310.60	194.10	177.80	161.70	145.60	712.10
6,400	405.60	378.60	351.60	324.50	202.80	185.80	169.00	152.10	737.10
6,800	424.10	395.90	367.60	339.30	212.10	194.30	176.70	159.10	762.30
7,200	446.00	416.30	386.60	356.80	223.00	204.30	185.80	167.30	788.90
7,600	465.60	434.60	403.60	372.50	232.80	213.30	194.00	174.60	814.70
8,000	482.60	450.50	418.30	386.10	241.30	221.10	201.10	181.00	844.50
8,400	492.90	460.10	427.20	394.40	246.50	225.80	205.40	184.90	862.60
8,800	505.10	471.50	437.80	404.10	252.60	231.40	210.50	189.50	883.80
9,200	516.00	481.60	447.20	412.80	258.00	236.40	215.00	193.50	903.00
9,400	520.40	485.80	451.10	416.40	260.20	238.40	216.80	195.20	910.40
9,600	524.60	489.70	454.70	419.70	262.30	240.30	218.50	196.80	918.00
9,800	530.40	495.10	459.70	424.40	265.20	243.00	221.00	198.90	928.00
10,000	534.70	499.10	463.50	427.80	267.40	245.00	222.80	200.60	935.70

[1] If a person is eligible for both a worker's benefit and a spouse's benefit, the check actually payable is limited to the larger of the two.

[2] The maximum amount payable to a family is generally reached when a worker and two family members are eligible.

APPENDIX

Appendix A

STATE-BY-STATE SUMMARY OF EFFECT OF DIVORCE ON MATRIMONIAL SUPPORT

Alabama: Fault is one of the bases on which court determines amount and recipient of support unless the divorce is granted on a "no fault" ground. Only the wife is eligible to receive support. There are no statutory provisions for the division of property.

Alaska: Fault is not taken into consideration in court's determination of the amount and recipient of support of the division of property. Either spouse is eligible to receive support or property.

Arizona: Fault is not taken into consideration in court determination of the amount and recipient of support or the division of property. Either spouse is eligible to receive support or property. Any community property or joint tenancy property not divided is kept by both spouses as tenants in common.

Arkansas: Fault is one of the bases on which court determines amount and recipient of support and division of property. Only the wife is eligible to receive support and property. Spouses may make a contract stipulating alimony payments and distribution of property; if approved by the court, the court will be enforceable.

California: Fault is not taken into consideration in court's determination of the amount and recipient of support or the division of property. Either spouse is eligible to receive support or property. Community property is divided equally. Spouses may make a contract stipulating support payments and distribution of property; if approved by the court, the contract will be enforceable.

Colorado: Fault is not taken into consideration in court's determination of the amount and recipient of support or the division of property. Either spouse is eligible to receive support or property. In the division of property, court may give preference to the spouse who has custody of couple's minor children.

Connecticut: Fault is not taken into consideration in court's determination of the amount and recipient of support or the division of property. Either spouse is eligible to receive support or property. Spouses may make a contract stipulating support payments, distribution of property, and child custody and support; if approved by the court, the contract will be enforced.

Delaware: Fault is not taken into consideration in court's determination of the amount and recipient of support or the division of property. Support will be granted to the defendant in a divorce case based on imcompatibility if he or she can prove dependence on the other spouse. Wife may be granted a reasonable share of husband's real and personal property if the divorce is not granted on grounds of incompatability, voluntary separation, or under age. Spouses may make a contract stipulating support payments and distribution of property; if approved by the court, the contract will be enforceable.

District of Columbia: Fault is not taken into consideration in court's determination of the amount and recipient of support or the division of property. Only the wife is eligible to receive support, but either spouse may be awarded property. Spouses may make a contract stipulating support payments and distribution of property; if approved by the court, the contract will be enforceable.

Florida: Fault is not taken into consideration in court's determination of the amount and recipient of support. Either spouse is eligible to receive support. There are no statutory provisions for the division of property.

Georgia: Fault is not taken into consideration in court's determination of the amount and recipient of support. Only the wife is eligible to receive support. There are no statutory provisions for division of property, except that joint tenancy is not affected by the divorce.

Hawaii: Fault is not taken into consideration in court's determination of the amount and recipient of support or the division of property. Either spouse is eligible to receive support or property. Spouses may-make a contract stipulating support payments and distribution of property; if approved by the court, the contract will be enforceable.

Idaho: Fault is one of the bases on which court determines amount and recipient of support unless the divorce is granted on a "no fault" ground. Only the wife is eligible to receive support. Either party may be awarded community property.

Illinois: Fault is not taken into consideration in court's determination of the amount and recipient of support or the division of property. Either spouse is eligible to receive support or property.

Indiana: Fault is not taken into consideration in court's determination of the amount and recipient of support or the division of property. Either spouse is eligible to receive support or property, although court may not award support payments unless the spouse is incapacitated, and then only for the duration of the disability. Spouses may make a contract stipulating support payments, distribution of property, and education and religious training of minor children; if approved by the court, the contract will be enforceable.

Iowa: Fault is not taken into consideration in court's determination of the amount and recipient of support or the division of property. Either spouse is eligible to receive support or property.

Kansas: Fault is not taken into consideration in court's determination of the amount and recipient of support or the division of property.

Kentucky: Fault is not taken into consideration in court's determination of the amount and recipient of support and the division of property. Either spouse is eligible to receive support or property. Spouses may make a contract stipulating support payments and distribution of property; if approved by the court, the contract will be enforceable.

Louisiana: Fault is one of the bases on which court determines amount and recipient of support and property. Only the wife is eligible to receive alimony, but either spouse may be awarded property. Community property is divided equally.

Maine: Fault is one of the bases on which court determines amount and recipient of support and division of property unless the divorce is granted on a "no fault" ground.

Only the wife is eligible to receive support, but either spouse may be awarded property.

Maryland: Fault is one of the bases on which court determines amount and recipient of support and division of property. Either spouse is eligible to receive support or property, but support is absolutely barred to a spouse guilty of adultery.

Massachusetts: Fault is not taken into consideration in court's determination; that not divided is kept by both spouses as tenants in common.

Michigan: Fault is not taken into consideration in court's determination of the amount and recipient of support or the division of property. Either spouse is eligible to receive support or property. Any joint tenancy property amount and recipient of support or the division of property. Either spouse is eligible to receive support of property. Any joint tenancy property not divided is kept by both spouses as tenants in common. Spouses may make a contract stipulating support payments and distribution of property; if approved by the court, the contract will be enforceable.

Minnesota: Fault is not taken into consideration in court's determination of the amount and recipient of support or the division of property. Either spouse is eligible to receive support property.

Mississippi: Fault is not taken into consideration in court's determination of the amount and recipient of support. Only the wife is eligible to receive support. There are no statutory provisions for division of property, except that joint tenancy is not affected by the divorce.

Missouri: Fault is not taken into consideration in court's determination of the amount and recipient of support or the division of property. Either spouse is eligible to receive support or property. Spouses may make a contract stipulating support payments, distribution of property, and child custody, support and visitation rights; if approved by the court, the contract will be enforceable.

Montana: Fault is one of the bases on which court determines amount and recipient of support and division of property. Only the wife is eligible to receive support, but either spouse may be awarded property. Spouses may make a contract stipulating support payments and distribution of property; if approved by the court, the contract will be enforceable.

Nebraska: Fault is not taken into consideration in court's determination of the amount and recipient of support or the division of property. Either spouse is eligible to receive support or property. Spouses may make a contract stipulating support payments, distribution of property, and child custody and support; if approved by the court, the contract will be enforceable.

Nevada: Fault is not taken into consideration in court's determination of the amount and recipient of support or the division of property. Only the wife is eligible to receive support and part of husband's separate property, but either spouse may be awarded community property. Spouses may make a contract stipulating support payments, distribution of property, and child custody and support; if approved by the court, the contract will be enforceable.

New Hampshire: Fault is one of the bases on which court determines amount and recipient of support and division of property unless divorce is granted on a "no fault" ground. Only the wife is eligible to receive support and property.

New Jersey: Fault is one of the bases on which court determines amount and recipient of support and division of property. Either spouse is eligible to receive support of property.

New Mexico: Fault is not taken into consideration in court's determination of the amount and recipient of support. Either spouse is eligible to receive support. There are no statutory provisions for the basis on which property is divided because the decree may not include a division of property; proceedings may be instituted later to have it divided, however. Spouses may make a contract stipulating support payments and distribution of property; if approved by the court, the contract will be enforceable.

New York: Fault is one of the bases on which court determines amount and recipient of support and division of property. Only wife is eligible to receive alimony and property.

North Carolina: Fault is one of the bases on which court determines amount and recipient of alimony. Either spouse is eligible to receive support, but it is absolutely barred to a spouse guilty of adultery. There are no statutory provisions for the basis on which property is divided.

North Dakota: Fault is not taken into consideration in court's determination of the amount and recipient of support or the division of property. Either spouse is eligible to receive support or property.

Ohio: Fault is one of the bases on which court determines amount and recipient of support and division of property. Either spouse is eligible to receive support or property.

Oklahoma: Fault is one of the bases on which court determines amount and recipient of support and division of property unless the divorce is granted on a "no fault" ground. Only the wife is eligible to receive support, but either spouse may be awarded property.

Oregon: Fault is not taken into consideration in court's determination of the amount and recipient of support or the division of property. Either spouse is eligible to receive support of property. Any joint tenancy property not divided is kept by both spouses as tenants in common. Spouses may make a contract stipulating support payments and distribution of property; if approved by the court, the contract will be enforceable.

Pennsylvania: Fault is one of the bases on which court determines amount and recipient of support, but there are no statutory provisions to grant it except to a wife during a legal separation or to either spouse if the divorce was granted on the grounds of insanity and the insane person's estate is not sufficient to provide his or her support. There are no statutory provisions for the basis on which property is divided, but any joint tenancy property not divided is kept by both spouses as tenants in common.

Rhode Island: Fault is one of the bases on which court determines amount and recipient of support and division of property. Only the wife is eligible to receive support, but ony if she has waived her dower rights, to which she is entitled upon divorce. Either spouse is eligible to receive property.

South Carolina: Fault is one of the bases on which court determines amount and recipient of support. Only the wife is eligible to receive support, but it is absolutely barred to her if she is guilty of adultery. There are no statutory provisions for the basis on which property is divided.

South Dakota: Fault is one of the bases on which court determines amount and recipient of support but it is not considered in the division of property. Only the wife is eligible to receive support, but either spouse may be awarded property.

Tennessee: Fault is one of the bases on which court determines amount and recipient of support but it is not considered in the division of property. Only the wife is eligible to receive support, but either spouse may be awarded property. Spouses may make a contract stipulating support payments and distribution of property; if approved by the court, the contract will be enforceable.

Texas: Fault is not taken into consideration in court's determination of the division of property.

Utah: Fault is not taken into consideration in court's determination of the amount and recipient of support or in the division of property. Either spouse is eligible to receive support or property.

Vermont: Fault is not taken into consideration in court's determination of the amount and recipient of support or the division of property. Either spouse is eligible to receive support, but only the wife may be awarded property.

Virginia: Fault is one of the bases on which court determines amount and recipient of support. Either spouse is eligible to receive support. There are no statutory provisions for the basis on which property is divided, but any joint tenancy property not divided is kept by both spouses as tenants in common. Spouses may make a contract stipulating support payments, distribution of property and child custody and support; if approved by the court, the contract will be enforceable.

Washington: Fault is not taken into consideration in court's determination of the amount and recipient of support or the division of property. Either spouse is eligible to receive support or property.

West Virginia: Fault is one of the bases on which court determines amount and recipient of support and division of property. Either spouse is eligible to receive support or property.

Wisconsin: Fault is one of the bases on which court determines amount and recipient of support but it is not considered in the division of property. Either spouse is eligible to receive support or property, but support is absolutely barred to a spouse guilty of adultery.

Wyoming: Fault is not taken into consideration in court's determination of the amount and recipient of support or the division of property. Only the wife is eligible to receive support and property. Spouses may make a contract stipulating support payments and distribution of property; if approved by the court, the contract will be enforceable.

Appendix B

RIGHT OF DOWER, CURTESY AND STATUTORY SUBSTITUTIONS

STATE	Husband	Wife
Alabama	Life estate in wife's real property and one-half of all personal property, absolutely	Life estate in 1/3 of husband's real property if husband survived by lineal descendants and life estate in 1/2 if not survived by lineal descendants
Alaska	Abolished	Abolished
Arizona	Abolished	Abolished
Arkansas	Life estate in 1/3 of wife's real property and 1/3 of all personal property absolutely [1]	Life estate in 1/3 of husband's real property and 1/3 of all personal property absolutely
California	None	None
Colorado	None	Abolished
Connecticut	None	None
Delaware	Abolished	Abolished
District of Columbia	Abolished	Abolished
Florida	Abolished	Abolished
Georgia	None	Abolished
Hawaii	Life estate in 1/3 of wife's real property and 1/3 of all personal property absolutely	Life estate in 1/3 of husband's real property and 1/3 of all personal property absolutely

STATE	Husband	Wife
Idaho	Abolished	None
Illinois	Abolished	Abolished
Indiana	Abolished	Abolished
Iowa	Abolished	Abolished
Kansas	One-half absolutely, of all wife's real property	One-half absolutely, of all husband's real property
Kentucky	Life estate in 1/3 of wife's real property	Life estate in 1/3 husband's real property
Louisiana	None	None
Maine	Abolished	Abolished
Maryland	Abolished	Abolished
Massachusetts	Life estate in 1/3 wife's real property	Life estate in 1/3 husband's real property
Michigan	Abolished	Life estate in 1/3 husband's real property
Minnesota	Abolished	Abolished
Mississippi	Abolished	Abolished
Missouri	Abolished	Abolished
Montana	None	Abolished
Nebraska	Abolished	Abolished
Nevada	Abolished	Abolished
New Hampshire	Abolished	Abolished
New Jersey	Life estate in 1/2 real property	Life estate in 1/2 husband's real property
New Mexico	None	None
New York	Abolished	Abolished

STATE	Husband	Wife
North Carolina	Abolished	Abolished
North Dakota	None	Abolished
Ohio	Life estate in 1/3 of wife's real property	Life estate in 1/3 of husband's real property
Oklahoma	Abolished	Abolished
Oregon	Abolished	Abolished
Pennsylvania	None	None
Rhode Island	Life estate in all wife's real property	Life estate in 1/3 of husband's real property
South Carolina	Abolished	Life estate in 1/3 of husband's real property
South Dakota	Abolished	Abolished
Tennessee	Life estate in all wife's real property	Life estate in 1/3 of husband's real property
Texas	None	None
Utah	Abolished	One-third, in value, of all husband's real property [3]
Vermont	One-third in value of wife's real property [4]	One-third in value of husband's real property [4]
Virginia	1/3 of wife's real property	1/3 of husband's real property
Washington	Abolished	Abolished
West Virginia	Life estate in 1/3 of wife's real property	Life estate in 1/3 of husband's real property

STATE	Husband	Wife
Wisconsin	Life estate in 1/3 of property owned by wife at death	Life estate in 1/3 of husband's real property
Wyoming	Abolished	Abolished

---

[1] Husband's interest may be defeated by will or conveyance by his wife.
[2] Wife takes a life estate in 1/3 husband's real property if marriage and ownership of property took place prior to September 1, 1930.
[3] See Uniform Probate Code, effective July 1, 1977 (75-1-101 et seq).
[4] Surviving spouse entitled to ½ in value of the real property if decedent was survived by issue or heir by adoption.

Appendix C

LIMIT OF VALUE OF HOMESTEAD

State	Limit of Value	Limit of Area
ALABAMA	$6,000 (widow or minor children) $2,000 (others)	160 acres
ALASKA	$12,000	1/4 acre in town or city, 160 acres elsewhere
ARIZONA	$15,000	None
ARKANSAS	$2,500	1/4 acre in city, town or village; 80 acres elsewhere
CALIFORNIA	$20,000 (head of family or over 65 years of age) $10,000 (others)	No limitation
COLORADO	$7,500	No limitation
FLORIDA	None	1/2 acre in city or town; 160 acres elsewhere
GEORGIA	$500 (in town or city) $200 (elsewhere)	50 acres outside of town or city
HAWAII	$20,000 (head of family or over 65 years of age) $10,000 (others)	1 acre in "one piece of land"
IDAHO	$10,000 (head of family) $4,000 (others)	No limitation
ILLINOIS	$10,000	No limitation
IOWA	$500	1/2 acre in city or town; 40 acres elsewhere
KANSAS	None	1 acre in city of town; 160 acres of farm land
KENTUCKY	$1,000	None
LOUISIANA	$15,000	160 acres

State	Limit of Value	Limit of Area
MAINE	$3,000	No limitation
MASSACHUSETTS	$30,000	No limitation
MICHIGAN	$3,500	1 lot in city, town or village; 40 acres elsewhere
MINNESOTA	None	1/3 acre in city, village or borough over 5,000 population; ½ acre if less than 5,000 population; 80 acres elsewhere
MISSISSIPPI	$5,00	160 acres
MISSOURI	$1,500 in country $3,000 in city in city	160 acres in country; 30 sq. rods to 5 acres in city (depending on population)
MONTANA	$2,500	¼ acre in city or town; 320 acres of agricultural land
NEBRASKA	$2,000	2 lots in city or village; 160 acres in country
NEVADA	$10,000	None
NEW HAMPSHIRE	$1,000	None
NEW JERSEY	$1,000	None
NEW MEXICO	$1,000	None
NEW YORK	$1,000	None
NORTH CAROLINA	$1,000	None
NORTH DAKOTA	$25,000 in town No limit in country.	2 acres in town; 160 acres in country

State	Limit of Value	Limit of Area
OHIO	$1,000	None
OKLAHOMA	$5,000	160 acres if rural
OREGON	$5,000	1 block in city; 160 acres elsewhere
PENNSYLVANIA	No law	—
RHODE ISLAND	No law	—
SOUTH CAROLINA	$1,000	None
TEXAS	$10,000 in city, town or village; no limit in rural areas	200 acres for family; 100 acres for single adult
UTAH	$4,000 plus $1,500 for wife and $600 for each other member of family	No limitation
VERMONT	$5,000	No limitation
VIRGINIA	$3,500	No limitation
WASHINGTON	$10,000	No limitation
WEST VIRGINIA	$1,000	No limitation
WISCONSIN	$25,000	40 acres of agricultural land; 1/4 acre otherwise
WYOMING	$4,000	No limitation

Appendix D

REVISED UNIFORM RECIPROCAL ENFORCEMENT OF SUPPORT ACT (1968)

PREFATORY NOTE

The above Act is the result of changes made in 1968 by the National Conference of Commissions on Uniform State Laws in the Uniform Reciprocal Enforcement of Support Act (as amended in 1958). Seven new section have been added to the former Act (Sections 11b, 20, 21, 24, 28, 35 and 39), substantial changes have been made in eight others (Sections 12, 15, 17, 18, 23, 38, 40 and 41) and lesser changes, to improve the style or clarify the meaning, have been made in others (Sections 1, 2, 9, 14, 25, 29, 30, 32 and 34). For these reasons the Conference decided to add the word "Revised" to the title of the Act.

The original Act was first approved and recommended for enactment in 1950. That Act was amended in 1952 and again in 1958. By 1957 it (or substantially similar act) had been passed in all States, the District of Columbia, the Commonwealth of Puerto Rico and most of the other areas subject to the jurisdiction of the United States such as the insular possessions.

The Act itself creates no duties of family support but leaves this to the legislatures of the several states. The Act is concerned solely with the enforcement of the already existing duties when the person to whom a duty is owed is in one state and the person owing the duty is in another state (or, under the Act as it has been adopted in a few states, is in a different county of the same state). * * *

The amendments of 1968, like previous ones, are designed to plug loop holes and cure defects in the enforcement procedure. Machinery for enforcement in many states is efficient. In a few states it is less so. Sometimes local officials have not fulfilled their duties. The present Act seeks to create ways and means of filling this gap (Sections 12, 18 and 29). Improved machinery for finding the obligor has been written into the Act (Section 17). The new Act has guidelines for the conduct of the trial in the responding state (Sections 21 and 23), for cases where paternity is in issue (Section 28) or where there has been interference with visitation rights (Section 24) or where it may be desirable to take an appeal (Section 35). The procedure for registering and enforcing out-of-state support orders has been simplified (Sections 40 and 41).

Part I — General Provisions

SECTION 1. [*Purposes.*] The purposes of this Act are to improve and extend by reciprocal legislation the enforcement of duties of support.

SECTION 2. [*Definitions.*]

(a) "Court" means the [here insert name] court of this State and when the context requires means the court of any other state as defined in a substantially similar reciprocal law.

(b) "Duty of support" means a duty of support whether imposed or imposable by law or by order, decree, or judgment of any court, whether interlocutory or final or whether incidental to an action for divorce, separation, separate maintenance, or otherwise and includes the duty to pay arrearages of support past due and unpaid.

(c) "Governor" includes any person performing the functions of Governor or the executive authority of any state covered by this Act.

(d) "Initiating state" means a state in which a proceeding pursuant to this or a substantially similar reciprocal law is commenced. "Initiating court" means the court in which a proceeding is commenced.

(e) "Law" includes both common and statutory law.

(f) "Obligee" means a person including a state or political subdivision to whom a duty of support is owed or a person including a state or political subdivision that has commenced a proceeding for enforcement of an alleged duty of support or for registration of a support order. It is immaterial if the person to whom a duty of support is owed is a recipient of public assistance.

(g) "Obligor" means any person owing a duty of support or against whom a proceeding for the enforcement of a duty of support or registration of a support order is commenced.

(h) "Prosecuting attorney" means the public official in the appropriate place who has the duty to enforce criminal laws relating to the failure to provide for the support of any person.

(i) "Register" means to [record] [file] in the Registry of Foreign Support Orders.

(j) "Registering court" means any court of this State in which a support order of a rendering state is registered.

(k) "Rendering state" means a state in which the court has issued a support order for which registration is sought or granted in the court of another state.

(l) "Responding state" means a state in which any responsive proceeding pursuant to the proceeding in the initiating state is commenced. "Responding court" means the court in which the responsive proceeding is commenced.

(m) "State" includes a state, territory, or possession of the United States, the District of Columbia, the Commonwealth of Puerto Rico, and any foreign jurisdiction in which this or a substantially similar reciprocal law is in effect.

(n) "Support order" means any judgment, decree, or order of support in favor of an obligee whether temporary or final, or subject to modification, revocation, or remission, regardless of the kind of action or proceeding in which it is entered.

SECTION 3. *[Remedies Additional to Those Now Existing.]* The remedies herein provided are in addition to and not in substitution for any other remedies.

SECTION 4. *[Extent of Duties of Support.]* Duties of support arising under the law of this State, when applicable under section 7, bind the obligor present in this State regardless of the presence or residence of the obligee.

Part II — Criminal Enforcement

SECTION 5. *[Interstate Rendition.]* The Governor of this State may

(1) demand of the Governor of another state the surrender of a person found in that state who is charged criminally in this State with failing to provide for the support of any person; or

(2) surrender on demand by the Governor of another state a person found in this State who is charged criminally in that state with failing to provide for the support of any person. Provisions for extradition of criminals not inconsistent with this Act apply to the demand even if the person whose surrender is demanded was not in the demanding state at the time of the commission of the crime and has not fled therefrom. The demand, the oath, and any proceedings for extradition pursuant to this section need not state or show that the person whose surrender is demanded has fled from justice or at the time of the commission of the crime was in the demanding state.

SECTION 6. *[Conditions of Interstate Rendition.]*

(a) Before making the demand upon the Governor of another state for the surrender of a person charged criminally in this State with failing to provide for the support of a person, the Governor of this State may require any prosecuting attorney of this State to satisfy him that at least [60] days prior thereto the obligee initiated proceedings for support under this Act or that any proceeding would be of no avail.

(b) If, under a substantially similar Act, the Governor of another state makes a demand upon the Governor of this State for the surrender of a person charged criminally in that state with failure to provide for the support of a person, the Governor may require any prosecuting attorney to investigate the demand and to report to him whether proceedings for support have been initiated or would be effective. If it appears to the Governor that a proceeding would be effective but has not been initiated he may delay honoring the demand for a reasonable time to permit the initiation of a proceeding.

(c) If proceedings have been initiated and the person demanded has prevailed therein the Governor may decline to honor the demand. If the obligee prevailed and the person demanded is subject to a support order, the Governor may decline to honor the demand if the person demanded is complying with the support order.

Part III — Civil Enforcement

SECTION 7. [*Choice of Law.*] Duties of support applicable under this Act are those imposed under the laws of any state where the obligor was present for the period during which support is sought. The obligor is presumed to have been present in the responding state during the period for which support is sought until otherwise shown.

SECTION 8. [*Remedies of State or Political Subdivision Furnishing Support.*] If a state or a political subdivision furnishes support to an individual obligee it has the same right to initiate a proceeding under this Act as the individual obligee for the purpose of securing reimbursement for support furnished and of obtaining continuing support.

SECTION 9. [*How Duties of Support Enforced.*] All duties of support, including the duty to pay arrearages, are enforcable by a proceeding under this Act including a proceeding for civil contempt. The defense that the parties are immune to suit because of their relationship as husband and wife or parent and child is not available to the obligor.

SECTION 10. [*Jurisdiction.*] Jurisdiction of any proceeding under this Act is vested in the [here insert title of court desired.]

SECTION 11. [*Contents and Filing of [Petition] for Support; Venue.*]

(a) The [petition] shall be verified and shall state the name and, so far as known to the obligee, the address and circumstances of the obligor and the persons for whom support is sought, and all other pertinent information. The obligee may include in or attach to the [petition] any information which may help in locating or identifying the obligor including a photograph of the obligor, a description of any distinguishing marks on his person, other names and aliases by which he has been or is known, the name of his employer, his fingerprints, and his Social Security number.

(b) The [petition] may be filed in the appropriate court of any state in which the obligee resides. The court shall not decline or refuse to accept and forward the [petition] on the ground that it should be filed with some other court of this or any other state where there is pending another action for divorce, separation, annulment, dissolution, habeas corpus, adoption, or custody between the same parties or where another court has already issued a support order in some other proceeding and has retained jurisdiction for its enforcement.

Comment

Wherever in this Act the word "petition" appears the word may be changed to "complaint" or "declaration" or the like and the word "petitioner" may be changed to "complainant" to conform to local usage.

SECTION 12. [*Officials to Represent Obligee.*] If this State is acting as an initiating state the prosecuting attorney upon the request of the court [a state department of welfare, a county commissioner, an overseer of the poor, or other local welfare officer] shall represent the obligee in any proceeding under this Act. [If the prosecuting attorney neglects or refuses to represent the obligee the [Attorney General] may order him to comply with the request of the court or may undertake the representation.] [If the prosecuting attorney neglects or refuses to represent the obligee, the [Attorney General] [State Director of Public Welfare] may undertake the representation.]

Comment

The first bracketed sentence is to be used in states where the Attorney General has supervisory powers over the prosecuting attorney; whereas, the second bracketed sentence is to be used if he does not have such powers.

SECTION 13. [*Petition for a Minor.*] A [petition] on behalf of a minor obligee may be executed and filed by a person having legal custody of the minor without appointment as guardian ad litem.

SECTION 14. *[Duty of Initiating Court.]* If the initiating court finds that the *[petition]* sets forth facts from which it may be determined that the obligor owes a duty of support and that a court of the responding state may obtain jurisdiction of the obligor or his property it shall so certify and cause 3 copies of the *[petition]* and its certificate and one copy of this Act to be sent to the responding court. Certification shall be in accordance with the requirements of the initiating state. If the name and address of the responding court is unknown and the responding state has an information agency comparable to that established in the initiating state it shall cause the copies to be sent to the state information agency or other proper official of the responding state, with a request that the agency or official forward them to the proper court and that the court of the responding state acknowledge their receipt to the initiating court.

SECTION 15. *[Costs and Fees.]* An initiating court shall not require payment of either a filing fee or other costs from the obligee but may request the responding court to collect fees and costs from the obligor. A responding court shall not require payment of a filing fee or other costs from the obligee but it may direct that all fees and costs requested by the initiating court and incurred in this State when acting as a responding state, including fees for filing of pleadings, service of process, seizure of property, stenographic or duplication service, or other service supplied to the obligor, be paid in whole or in part by the obligor or by the [state or political subdivision thereof.] These costs or fees do not have priority over amounts due to the obligee.

SECTION 16. *[Jurisdiction by Arrest.]* If the court of this State believes that the obligor may flee it may

(1) as an initiating court, request in its certificate that the responding court obtain the body of the obligor by appropriate process; or

(2) as a responding court, obtain the body of the obligor by appropriate process. Thereupon it may release him upon his own recognizance or upon his giving a bond in an amount set by the court to assure his appearance at the hearing.

SECTION 17. *[State Information Agency.]*

(a) The [Attorney General's Office, State Attorney's Office, Welfare Department or other Information Agency] is designated as the state information agency under this Act, it shall

(1) compile a list of the courts and their addresses in this State having jurisdiction under this Act and transmit it to the state information agency of every other state which has adopted this or a substantially similar Act. Upon the adjournment of each session of the [legislature] the agency shall distribute copies of any amendments to the Act and a statement of their effective date to all other state information agencies;

(2) maintain a register of lists of courts received from other states and transmit copies thereof promptly to every court in this state having jurisdiction under this Act; and

(3) forward to the court in this State which has jurisdiction over the obligor or his property petitions, certificates and copies of the Act it receives from courts or information agencies of other states.

(b) If the state information agency does not know the location of the obligor or his property in the state and no state location service is available it shall use all means at its disposal to obtain this information, including the examination of official records in the state and other sources such as telephone directories, real property records, vital statistics records, police records, requests for the name and address from employers who are able or willing to cooperate, records of motor vehicle license offices, requests made to the tax offices both state and federal where such offices are able to cooperate, and requests made to the Social Security Administration as permitted by the Social Security Act as amended.

(c) After the deposit of 3 copies of the [petition] and certificate and one copy of the Act of the initiating state with the clerk of the appropriate court, if the state information agency knows or believes that the prosecuting attorney is not prosecuting the case diligently it shall inform the [Attorney General] [State Director of Public Welfare,] who may undertake the representation.

SECTION 18. [*Duty of the Court and Officials of This State as Responding State.*]

(a) After the responding court receives copies of the [petition], certificate and Act from the initiating court the clerk of the court shall docket the case and notify the prosecuting attorney of his action.

(b) The prosecuting attorney shall prosecute the case diligently. He shall take all action necessary in accordance with the laws of this State to enable the court ot obtain jurisdiction over the obligor or his property and shall request the court [clerk of the court] to set a time and place for a hearing and give notice thereof to the obligor in accordance with law.

(c) [If the prosecuting attorney neglects or refuses to represent the obligee the [Attorney General] may order him to comply with the request of the court or may undertake the representation.] [If the prosecuting attorney neglects or refuses to represent the obligee, the [Attorney General] [State Director of Public Welfare] may undertake the representation.]

Comment

The first bracketed sentence is to be used in states where the Attorney General has supervisory powers over the prosecuting attorney; whereas, the second bracketed sentence is to be used if he does not have such powers.

SECTION 19. [*Further Duties of Court and Officials in the Responding State.*]

(a) The prosecuting attorney on his own initiative shall use all means at his disposal to locate the obligor or his property, and if because of inaccuracies in the [petition] or otherwise the court cannot obtain jurisdiction the prosecuting attorney shall inform the court of what he has done and request the court to continue the case pending receipt of more accurate information or an amended [petition] from the initiating court.

(b) If the obligor or his property is not found in the [county], and the prosecuting attorney discovers that the obligor or his property may be found in another [county] of this State or in another state he shall so inform the court. Thereupon the clerk of the court shall forward the documents received from the court in the initiating state to a court in the other [county] or to a court in the other state or to the information agency or other proper official of the other state with a request that the documents be forwarded to the proper court. All powers and duties provided by this Act apply to the receipient of the documents so forwarded. If the clerk of a court of this State forwards documents to another court he shall forthwith notify the initiating court.

(c) If the prosecuting attorney has no information as to the location of the obligor or his property he shall so inform the initiating court.

SECTION 20. [*Hearing and Continuance.*] If the obligee is not present at the hearing and the obligor denies owing the duty of support alleged in the petition or offers evidence constituting a defense the court, upon request of either party, continue the hearing to permit evidence relative to the duty to be adduced by either party by deposition or by appearing in person before the court. The court may designate the judge of the initiating court as a person before whom a deposition may be taken.

SECTION 21. [*Immunity from Criminal Prosecuton.*] If at the hearing the obligor is called for examination as an adverse party and he declines to answer upon the ground that his testimony may tend to incriminate him, the court may require to answer, in which event he is immune from criminal prosecution with respect to matters revealed by his testimony, except for perjury committed in this testimony.

SECTION 22. [*Evidence of Husband and Wife.*] Laws attaching a privilege against the disclosure of communications between husband and wife are inapplicable to proceedings under this Act. Husband and wife are competent witnesses *[and may be compelled]* to testify to any relevant matter, including marriage and parentage.

SECTION 23. [*Rules of Evidence.*] In any hearing for the civil enforcement of this Act the court is governed by the rules of evidence applicable in a civil court action in the ____,____,____ Court. If the action is based on a support order issued by another court a certified copy of the order shall be received as evidence of the duty of support, subject only to any defenses available to an obligor with respect to paternity [Section 27] or to a defendant in an action or a proceeding to enforce a foreign money judgment. The determination or enforcement of a duty of support owed to one obligee is unaffected by any interference by another obligee with rights of custody or visitation granted by a court.

SECTION 24. [*Order of Support.* If the responding court finds a duty of support it may order the obligor to furnish support or reimbursement therefor and subject the property of the obligor to the order. Support orders made pursuant to this Act shall require that payments be made to the [clerk] [bureau][probation department] of the court of the responding state. [The court and prosecuting attorney of any [county] in which the obligor is present or has property have the same powers and duties to enforce the order as have those of the [county] in which it was first issued. If enforcement is impossible or cannot be completed in the [county] in which the order was issued, the prosecuting attorney shall send a certified copy of the order to the prosecuting attorney of any [county] in which it appears that proceedings to enforce the order would be effective. The prosecuting attorney to whom the certified copy of the order is forwarded shall proceed with enforcement and report the results of the proceedings to the court first issuing the order.]

SECTION 25. [*Responding Court to Transmit Copies to Initiating Court.*] The responding court shall cause a copy of all support orders to be sent to the initiating court.

SECTION 26. [*Additional Powers of Responding Court.*] In addition to the foregoing powers a responding court may subject the obligor to any terms and conditions proper to assure compliance with its orders and in particular to:

(1) require the obligor to furnish a cash deposit or a bond of a character and amount to assure payment of any amount due;

(2) require the obligor to report personally and to make payments at specified intervals to the [clerk][bureau][probation department] of the court; and

(3) punish under the power of contempt the obligor who violates any order of the court.

SECTION 27. [*Paternity.*] If the obligor asserts as a defense that he is not the father of the child for whom support is sought and it appears to the court that the defense is not frivolous, and if both of the parties are present at the hearing or the proof required in the case indicates that the presence of either or both of the parties is not necessary, the court may adjudicate the paternity issue. Otherwise the court may adjourn the hearing until the paternity issue has been adjudicated.

SECTION 28. [*Additional Duties of Responding Court.*] A responding court has the following duties which may be carried out through the [clerk] [bureau] [Probation department] of the court:

(1) to transmit to the initiating court any payment made by

the obligor pursuant to any order of the court or otherwise; and

(2) to furnish to the initiating court upon request a certified statement of all payments made by the obligor.

SECTION 29. *[Additional Duty of Initiating Court.]* An initiating court shall receive and disburse forthwith all payments made by the obligor or sent by the responding court. This duty may be carried out through the [clerk] [bureau] [probation department] of the court.

SECTION 30. *[Proceedings Not to be Stayed.]* A responding court shall not stay the proceeding or refuse a hearing under this Act because of any pending or prior action or proceeding for divorce, separation, annulment, dissolution, habeas corpus, adoption, or custody in this or any other state. The court shall hold a hearing and may issue a support order pendente lite. In aid thereof it may require the obligor to give a bond for the prompt prosecution of the pending proceeding. If the other action or proceeding is concluded before the hearing in the instant proceeding and the judgment therein provides for the support demanded in the [petition] being heard the court must conform its support order to the amount allowed in the other action or proceeding. Thereafter the court shall not stay enforcement of its support order because of the retention of jurisdiction for enforcement purposes by the court in the other action or proceeding.

SECTION 31. *[Application of Payments.]* A support order made by a court of this State pursuant to this Act does not nullify and is not nullified by a support order made by a court of this State pursuant to any other law or by a support order made by a court of any other state pursuant to a substantially similar act or any other law, regardless of priority of issuances, unless otherwise specifically provided by the court. Amounts paid for a particular period pursuant to any support order made by the court of another state shall be credited against the amounts accruing or accrued for the same period under any support order made by the court of this State.

[SECTION 32. *[Effect of Participation in Proceeding.]* Participation in any proceeding under this Act does not confer jurisdiction upon any court over any of the parties thereto in any other proceeding.]

SECTION 33. *[Intrastate Application.]* This Act applies if

both the obligee and the obligor are in this State but in different [counties.] If the court of the [county] in which the [petition] is filed finds that the [petition] sets forth facts from which it may be determined that the obligor owes a duty of support and finds that a court of another [county] in this State may obtain jurisdiction over the obligor or his property, the clerk of the court shall send the [petition] and a certification of the findings to the court of the [county] in which the obligor or his property is found. The clerk of the court of the [county] receiving these documents shall notify the prosecuting attorney of their receipt. The prosecuting attorney and the court in the [county] to which the copies are forwarded then shall have duties corresponding to those imposed upon them when acting for this State as a responding state.]

SECTION 34. [*Appeals.*] If the [Attorney General] [State Director of Public Welfare] is of the opinion that a support order is erroneous and presents a question of law warranting an appeal in the public interest, he may

(a) perfect an appeal to the proper appellate court if the support order was issued by a court of this State, or

(b) if the support order was issued in another state, cause the appeal to be taken in the other state. In either case expenses of appeal may be paid on his order from funds appropriated for his office.

Part IV — Registration of Foreign Support Orders

SECTION 35. [*Additional Remedies.*] If the duty of support is based on a foreign support order, the obligee has the additional remedies provided in the following sections.

Comment

The language of the last sentence is permissive and so does not preclude other arrangements for the payment of the expenses of appeal. If it is thought desirable to spell out particular methods of payment this may be done.

SECTION 36. [*Registration.*] The obligee may register the foreign support order in a court of this State in the manner, with the effect, and for the purposes herein provided.

SECTION 37. [*Registry of Foreign Support Orders.*] The clerk of the court shall maintain a Registry of Foreign Support Orders in which he shall [file] foreign support orders.

SECTION 38. [*Official to Represent Obligee.*] If this State is acting either as a rendering or a registering state the prosecuting attorney upon the request of the court [a state department of welfare, a county commissioner, and overseer of the poor, or other local welfare official] shall represent the obligee in proceedings under this Part.

[If the prosecuting attorney neglects or refuses to represent the obligee, the [Attorney General] may order him to comply with the request of the court or may undertake the representation.] [If the prosecuting attorney neglects or refuses to represent the obligee, the [Attorney General] [State Director of Public Welfare] may undertake the representation.]

Comment

The first bracketed sentence is to be used in states where the Attorney General has supervisory powers over the prosecuting attorney; whereas, the second bracketed sentence is to be used if he does not have such powers.

SECTION 39. [*Registration Procedure; Notice.*]

(a) An obligee seeking to register a foreign support order in a court of this State shall transmit to the clerk of the court (1) three certified copies of the order with all modifications thereof, (2) one copy of the reciprocal enforcement of support act of the state in which the order was made, and (3) a statement verified and signed by the obligee, showing the post office address of the obligee, the last known place of residence and post office address of the obligor, the amount of support remaining unpaid, a description and the location of any property of the obligor available upon execution, and a list of the states in which the order is registered. Upon receipt of these documents the clerk of the court, without payment of a filing fee or other cost to the obligee, shall file them in the Registry of Foreign Support Orders. The filing constitutes registration under this Act.

(b) Promptly upon registration the clerk of the court shall send by certified or registered mail to the obligor at the address given a notice of the registration with a copy of the registered support order and the post office address of the obligee. He shall also docket the case and notify the prosecuting attorney of his action. The prosecuting attorney shall proceed diligently to enforce the order.

SECTION 40. *[Effect of Registration; Enforcement Procedure.]*

(a) Upon registration the registered foreign support order shall be treated in the same manner as a support order issued by a court of this State. It has the same effect and is subject to the same procedures, defenses, and proceedings for reopening, vacating, or staying as a support order of this State and may be enforced and satisfied in like manner.

(b) The obligor has [20] days after the mailing of notice of the registration in which to petition the court to vacate the registration or for other relief. If he does not so petition the registered support order is confirmed.

(c) At the hearing to enforce the registered support order the obligor may present only matters that would be available to him as defenses in an action to enforce a foreign money judgment. If he shows to the court that an appeal from the order is pending or will be taken or that a stay of execution has been granted the court shall stay enforcement of the order until the appeal is concluded, the time for appeal has expired, or the order is vacated, upon satisfactory proof that the obligor has furnished security for payment of the support ordered as required by the rendering state. If he shows to the court any ground upon which enforcement of a support order of this State may be stayed the court shall stay enforcement of the order for an appropriate period if the obligor furnishes the same security for payment of the support ordered that is required for a support order of this State.

SECTION 41. *[Uniformity of Interpretation.]* This Act shall be so construed as to effectuate its general purpose to make uniform the law of those states which enact it.

SECTION 42. *[Short Title.]* This Act may be cited as the Revised Uniform Reciprocal Enforcement of Support Act (1968).

SECTION 43. *[Severability.]* If any provision of this Act or the application thereof to any person or circumstance is held invalid, the invalidity does not affect other provisions or applications of the Act which can be given effect without the invalid provision or application, and to this end the provisions of this Act are severable.

Appendix E

SAMPLE SEPARATION AGREEMENT

THIS AGREEMENT made between Richard Roe, residing at 17 East 89th Street, Borough of Manhattan, City, County and State of New York, hereinafter referred to as the Husband and Mary Roe, residing at 95 Christopher Street, Borough of Manhattan, City, County and State of New York, hereinaafter referred to as the wife.

WITNESSETH:

WHEREAS the parties married on or about the 10th day of June, 1920, at Albany, New York, and there has been issue of the marriage, namely, James, born on the 29th day of October, 1925 and Marjorie, born on the 4th day of June, 1928, the children being sometimes hereinafter referred to as the Children; and

WHEREAS in consequence of disputes and unhappy differences, the parties have separated, and are now and for some time have been living apart, and since their separation have agreed to live separate and apart during their natural lives; and

WHEREAS the parties are desirous of settling their property rights and the question of the custody of the Children, and the Husband is desirous of making provisions for the maintenance, support and education of the Children, the welfare of the Children being the primary concern of the parties;

NOW THEREFORE, in consideration of the premises and the mutual promises and undertakings herein contained, and for other good and valuable considerations, the parties agree:

1. The parties may and shall at all times hereafter live and continue to live separate and apart. Each shall be free from interference, authority and control, direct or indirect, by the other as fully as if he is or she were sole and unmarried. Each may reside at such place or places as he or

she may select. Each may, for his or her separate use and benefit, conduct, carry on, and engage in any business, profession or employment which to him or her may seem advisable.

2. The parties shall not molest or interfere with each other, nor shall either of them compel or attempt to compel the other to cohabit or dwell with him or her. by any means whatsoever.

3. The Husband acknowledges that he is indebted to the Wife in the sum of................... He has simultaneously herewith executed and delivered to the Wife a certain collateral promissory note in like amount. The Wife hereby acknowledges receipt of the note.

4. The parties do hereby make the following division and settlement of their property:

(a) All the personal property of the parties (including furniture, furnishing, household effects and the like now located in the apartment formerly occupied by the parties or 95 Christopher Street, City of New York, State of New York, shall constitute the property of the Wife. The Husband shall and does hereby relinquish all right, title and interest that he may have therein. Notwithstanding the foregoing, the Wife shall permit the Husband to remove from the aforesaid apartment such personal belongings (including clothing, books, letters and the like) as the Husband may desire, and these shall constitute the property of the Husband. The Wife hereby acknowledges that all or substantially all the personal property which she is to receive under the provisions of this subdivision constituted the property of the Husband prior to the execution of this agreement; and that tsuch property is of considerable value.

(b) Except as herein provided to the contrary, each party shall own, have and enjoy independently of any claim or right of the other party, all personal and real property belonging to him or her, and now in his or her possession, or which may hereafter belong to him or her, with full power of disposition during lifetime or after death as though he or she were unmarried.

5. The real property located at Cornwall, County of Orange, State of New York, legal title to which now resides in the Wife, shall remain the sole and exclusive property of the Wife, free and clear of any claim on the part of the Husband. In consideration of the foregoing, the Wife hereby expressly agrees that (a) she shall not, during her lifetime, sell or otherwise dispose of the aforesaid real property unless compelled to do so by necessity; and (b) that barring such necessity, she shall make appropriate testamentary disposition so that the aforesaid real property shall pass to the Children upon her death, or if both of the Children predecease her, to the Husband.

6. The Will shall have custody of the Children, and control and supervision of their upbringing, subject to the following:

(a) The Husband shall have the right to visit the Children at any time on reasonable notice, and the Wife shall afford the Husband the opportunity to do so. Should it be found inconvenient by the Wife, for any reason, to have the Husband visit the Children, the Wife shall have the right and option to send the Children to the Husband in lieu of such visit.

(b) In addition, the Husband may at his option have the custody of the Children or any of them for (1) alternate week-ends (consisting of Saturday and Sunday) and also (2) during either the Christmas or Easter school vacation, and also (3) during one month of the summer school vacation.

(c) Whenever the Husband shall exercise any of his rights under this paragraph, he shall give reasonable notice to the Wife.

(d) Nothing herein contained, however, shall be construed as an obligation or a duty on the part of the Husband to accept custody of the Children or any of them at the time and for the periods herein indicated. The intention of the parties is that the Husband's partial custody shall be entirely optional with him; and should the Husband so desire, he may waive the privilege of partial custody on any occasion and for any reason, but without waiving his right to insist thereafter upon compliance with the provisions of this paragraph.

7. The Wife shall support and maintain herself, and shall in all respects care for, educate, maintain and support the Children properly and in such manner as to agord the Children the best care, education, maintenance, and support consistent with the payments made by the Husband in accordance with the terms of this agreement. In consideration thereof, the Husband shall make the following payments to the Wife:

(a) The sum of $200. per month for the support and maintenance of the Wife and for the support, maintenance and education of the Children. If one Child dies or becomes 25, this amount shall be reduced to $150. per month. If both Children die or become 25, it shall be reduced to $100. per month; and shall continue for the life of the Wife.

(b) The obligation of the Husband with respect to the amounts payable by him hereunder shall survive his death and shall constitute a charge upon his estate. In order to facilitate the administration of the Husband's estate, his legal representatives shall cause the President of the Society of Accountants of the City of New York to determine the capital sum to be set aside from the Husband's estate, the income of which will be sufficient to pay the amounts above specified. The proceeds of all policies of insurance carried by the Husband covering his life and payable to the Wife and/or the Children as beneficiaries, shall be utilized in making up such capital sum, and that in setting aside such capital sum, the estate of the Husband shall contribute only the difference between the aggregate amount required for payments hereunder, less the proceeds of such life insurance policies.

8. As long as the child James is alive and under the age

of twenty-one, the Husband shall keep in full force and effect insurance covering his own life, in a principal amount not less than $25,000., for the benefit of the child James. As long as the child Marjorie is alive and under the age of twenty-one, and is unmarried, the Husband shall keep in full force and effect insurance covering his own life, in a principal amount not less than $25,000., for the benefit of the child Marjorie.

9. The Husband shall forthwith make and keep in full force and effect until his death a will bequeathing and devising to the Children not less than one-third of his entire estate.

10. The counsel fees of the Wife, amounting to $500. have been paid simultaneously herewith by the Husband to the Wife's attorneys, Reilly & Reilly, Esqs., with offices at 500 Fifth Avenue, New York, N. Y., who have accepted the same in full payment of their services in connection with the preparation of this agreement, and all negotiations prior thereto.

11. The Wife accepts the provisions herein made for her in lieu of and in full settlement and satisfaction of any and all claims and rights against the Husband for her support and maintenance and for the support, maintenance, and education of the Children, and in full settlement and satisfaction of any and all other claims and rights whatsoever (including, but not by way of limitation, dower and all rights under the laws of testacy and intestacy), which she ever had, now has, or might hereafter have against the Husband by reason of their relationship as husband and wife, or otherwise. The Wife hereby releases and acquits the Husband and his estate of and from any and all claims, liabilities, and obligations whatsoever, except only suc has are specifically assumed by or imposed upon the Husband hereunder. It is the intention of the parties that except as otherwise provided herein, all liability of whatsoever nature on the part of the Husband to the Wife, past, present, and future, actual or potential, whether arising from their relationship as husband and wife or other-

wise, shall cease and terminate absolutely and forever. The Wife warrants to the Husband that she not heretofore incurred any obligations whatsoever for which the Husband or his estate may be or may become liable. Should any such obligations arise, the Husband shall have the right to deduct the amount thereof, together with all incidental expenses incurred by him, from the payments to be made by him to the Wife hereunder. So long as the Husband shall duly perform the terms and conditions of this agreement on his part to be performed, the Wife shall not at any time hereafter incur any debt or incur any obligation for which the Husband or his estate may be or may become liable; and the Wife shall at all times hereafter, so long as the Husband shall duly make the payments herein provided for, keep the Husband and his estate free and harmless from any and all debts and obligations.

12. If the Husband defaults in the due performance of any of the terms, conditions, and covenants of this agreement on his part to be performed, the Wife shall have the right, at her election, to sue for damages for the breach of this agreement, or to bring an action for a legal separation or for support and maintenance. Nothing herein contained shall in such event abrogate or restrict or otherwise affect the right of the Wife to exercise her aforesaid election.

13. Except as herein to the contrary provided, the parties shall and do hereby mutually remise, release, and forever discharge each other from any and all actions, suits, debts, claims, demands and obligations whatsoever, both in law and in equity, which either of them ever had, now has, or may hereafter have against the other upon or by reason of any matter, cause, or tnihg up to the date of the execution of this agreement, it being the intention of the parties that henceforth there shall be, as between them, only such rights and obligations as are specifically provided in this agreement.

14. Each party shall, (at the request and expense of the other party), at any time and from time to time hereafter,

take any and all steps and execute and deliver to the other party any and all instruments and assurances that the other party may reasonably require for the purpose of giving full force and effect to the provisions of this agreement.

15. Each party releases and relinquishes any and all claims and rights that he or she may have had, may now have, or may hereafter acquire (a) to share in any capacity or to any extent whatsoever in the estate of the other party upon the latter's death, whether by way of statutory allowance, or distribution in intestacy, or election to take against the other party's last will and testament under Section 18 of the Decedent Estate Law of the State of New York or otherwise; and, or (b) to act as executor or administrator of the other party's estate. It is the intention of the parties that this provision shall serve as a mutual waiver of the right of election, in accordance with the requirements of subdivision 9 of Section 18 of the Decedent Estate Law.

16. No modification or waiver of any of the terms of this agreement shall be valid unless in writing and executed with the same formality as this agreement. No waiver of any breach or default hereunder shall be deemed a waiver of any subsequent breach or default of the same or similar nature.

17. In the event of any dispute or misunderstanding arising out of or in connection with this agreement, such dispute or misunderstanding shall be arbitrated by the parties before some qualified person who shall be properly experienced in the subject-matter of the controversy, and, who shall be acceptable to both parties. Should the parties fail to agree upon such person, each party shall appoint an arbitrator, and the two arbitrators shall choose a third. The cost of the arbitration shall be borne as the arbitrator or arbitrators may direct. The decision of the arbitrator, or of the majority of the arbitrators, as the case may be, shall be binding and conclusive on the parties, and shall be rendered in such form that judgment may be entered thereon in the highest court of the forum having jurisdiction thereof.

18. The provisions of this agreement shall not be construed to prevent either party from suing for an absolute or limited divorce in this or any other competent jurisdiction upon such grounds as they shall elect or as they may be advised; but no decree so obtained by either party shall in any way affect this agreement or any of the terms, covenants, or conditions hereof, this agreement being absolute, unconditional, and irrevocable and both parties intending to be legally bound hereby.

19. All matters affecting the interpretation of this agreement and the rights of the parties hereto in relation to the children shall be governed by the laws of the State of New York.

20. The parties have incorporated in this agreement their entire understanding. No oral statement or prior written matter extrinsic to this agreement shall have any force or effect. The parties are not relying upon any representations other than those expressly set forth herein.

21. The parties hereto declare that each has had independent legal advice by counsel of his or her own selection; that each fully understands the facts and has been fully informed of all legal rights and liabilities; that after such advice, and knowledge, each believes the agreement to be fair, just and reasonable; and that each signs the agreement freely and voluntarily.

IN WITNESS WHEREOF the parties have set their hands and seals to four counterparts of this agreement, each of which shall constitute an original, this 19th day of October, 1937, in the City of New York, State of New York.

(Signed) Richard Roe (L.S.)

(Signed) Mary Roe (L.S.)

Witnessed by:

John Green (Signed)—As to the Husband

Jacob White (Signed)—As to the Wife

Reprinted by permission rfmo Horowitz, J. I. Manual of Divorce and other matrimonial actions. . . . in New York State, N. Y. Central Law Book Company, 1938.

Appendix F

SUPPORT OF PAUPER RELATIVES

Alabammaa	F, M, C, B, GF, GM, GC
Arkansas	F, M, C, GC
California	F, M, C,
Colorado	F, M, C, S, B, GF, GM, GC
Connecticut	F, M, C, B, GF, GM, GC
Georgia	F, M, C,
Idaho	F, M, C,
Illinois	F, M, C, S, B, GF, GM, GC
Indiana	C,
Iowa	F, M, C, GF, GM, GC
Kansas	F, M, C,
Kentucky	C,
Maine	F, M, C, GF, GM, GC
Maryland	F, M, C,
Massachusetts	C,
Michigan	F, M, C, GF, GM, GC
Minnesota	F, M, C, S, B, GF, GM, GC
Mississippi	F, M, C, S, B, GF, GM, GC
Montana	F, M, C, S, B, GF, GM, GC
Nebraska	F, M, C, S, B, GF, GM, GC
North Dakota	F, M, C,
New Jersey	F, M, C, GF, GM, GC
Oklahoma	F, M, C,
Oregon	F, M, C,
Pennsylvania	F, M, C,
Rhode Island	F, M, C, GF, GM, GC
South Dakota	F, M, C,
Utah	F, M, C, S, B, GF, GM, GC
Virginia	C,
Washington	F, M, C, S, B, GF, GM, GC
West Virginia	F, M, C, B, S,
Wisconsin	F, M, C,

Pauper Relatives must be supported by:
- F father of the pauper
- M mother
- C adult child
- B brother
- S sister
- GF grandfather
- GM grandmother
- GC grandchild

Appendix G

FORM: AGREEMENT TO FURNISH SUPPORT

Agreement made _____, 19____, between _____ A.B./, of _____/address/ City of _____, County of _____, State of _____, and /C.D./ of _____/address/ City of _____, County of _____, State of _____.

RECITALS

1. _____/A.B./ is advanced in years, _____/requires constant care and attention/ and is unable to support _____/himself *or* herself/ properly.

2. _____/C.D./ is willing and able to provide support for _____/A.B./.

3. _____/A.B./ desires to compensate _____ / C.D./ for the _____/care and/ support to be furnished under this agreement.

THE PARTIES AGREE AS FOLLOWS:

A. /C.D./ shall from this date until the date of the death of _____/A.B./ furnish to _____/A.B./, at the cost and expense of _____/C.D./, a comfortable home with a private room(s) for the use of _____/A.B./, and all necessaries of life suitable to the age and condition of _____/A.B./ including all required meals and clothing.

B. _____/C.D./ shall assume liability for and discharge all of the following monthly expenses of _____ of charge all of the following monthly expenses of _____/ A.B./: _____/*list expenses*/. In addition, _____ /C.D./ shall pay _____ Dollars ($_____) per month to _____/A.B./ for and as an allowance for incidental and personal expenses. Payment shall be made on the _____ day of each month, commencing on _____, 19____. The Assumption of expenses and monthly payments shall continue until the death of _____ /A.B./ or the death of _____ /C.D./, whichever first occurs.

4. _____ /C.D./ shall assume responsibility and pay all expenses for medicine and medical attendance of _____ /A.B./ including all expenses of the last illness of _____ / A.B./, as well as all expenses of a proper funeral and burial, to the extent that all such expenses are not covered by any private or public health or death insurance benefits to which _____ /A.B./ may be entitled.

5. As consideration for the care and support to be provided by _____ /C.D./ _____ /A.B./ shall convey to _____ ____ /C.D./ by _____ / *indicate type of deed*/ deed, real property in the County of _____, State of _____, described as follows: _____ /*set forth legal description*/, and shall transfer to _____ /C.D./ the following-described personal property: _____ / *set forth legal description*/: The conveyance and transfer shall occur on _____, 19____. If _____ /C.D./ shall or decease _____ /A.B./, and shall die within _____ years, then _____ /A.B./ shall receive _____ Dollars ($____) from the estate of _____ /C.D./ as further consideration for the conveyance of the real property.

6. The failure of _____ /C.D./ to provide the care and support required under the terms of this agreement shall render the conveyance of property provided for in Section Four of this agreement null and void. In the event of such failure, _____ /title to the property shall immediately revert to _____ /A.B./ without the necessity of any act on the part of _____ /A.B./ *or* /A.B. shall have the lawful right to re-enter and take possession of such property./

7. _____ /A.B./ shall reside at the home of _____ /C.D./ in the County of _____, State of _____, or wherever else _____ /C.D./ shall choose to establish a home.

8. Notwithstanding the requirement of Section Six of this agreement, _____ (A.B./ may refuse to reside at the home of _____ /C.D./ because of the neglect or inability of _____ /C.D./ to obtain comfortable and sufficient clothing, lodging, and maintenance for _____ /A.B./ shall rightfully elect not to live at the home of _____ /C.D./ shall not exceed the sum of _____ Dollars ($____) per month during the time of the rightful refusal of _____ (A.B. to live in the home of _____ (C.D.).

9. _____ /A.B./ may elect to terminate this agreement by paying to _____ /C.D./ a reasonable amount for _____/ his *or* her/board and care from the effective date to the day of termination of this agreement. The amount to be so paid shall be mutally agreed on, and, in the event of a failure to arrive at an agreement, the parties shall abide by the judgment of a board of arbitrators consisting of three members, one to be chosen by each party and a third member to be chosen by the two so designed.

10. This agreement is a personal contract solely for the benefit of _____ /A.B./ and is not intended for the benefit of any other person. The support to be furnished _____ /A.B./ under Section One of this agreement shall not be delegated to any other person by _____ /C.D./ by reason of any assignment or otherwise. This agreement shall become null and void on the death of _____ /A.B./ except as to liabilities expressly assumed by _____ /C.D./ hereunder.

In witness whereof, the parties have executed this agreement at _____ /*designate place of execution*/the day and year first above written.

/*Signatures*/

Appendix H

FORM: AGREEMENT BETWEEN PARENT AND CHILD FOR SUPPORT

Agreement made _____, 19____, between _____ /child/ and _____/parent/ the _____ (mother/ _____ of _____/child/.

A. _____/Parent/ is advanced in years, _____/ requires constant care and attention/, and is unable to provide support _____/herself/ properly.

B. _____/Child is willing and able to provide support for the _____/parent/.

C. _____/Parent/ desires to compensate _____ /child/ for the _____/care and/ support to be furnished under this agreement.

THE PARTIES AGREE AS FOLLOWS:

1. *Room and Board.* _____ /Child/ shall provide _____ _____ /parent/ with room and board in the home of _____/child/ at _____/address/ for as long as _____/parent/ lives. The room and board to be provided shall consist of (1) private use of the following room(s) in the home of _____/child/: _____; (2) shared use of the remainder of the house, with the exception of _____; (3) all meals; and (4) _____Dollars ($_____) per month as an allowance for incidentals and personal expenses.

2. *Last illness and funeral.* _____/Child/ shall assume responsibility for and pay all expenses of the last illness of _____/parent/, as well as all such expenses are not covered by any private or public health or death insurance benefits to which _____/parent/ may be entitled.

3. *Consideration.* _____/As consideration for the support to be furnished by _____/child/. _____/parent/ will pay _____/child _____Dollars ($_____) on execution of this agreement, receipt of which sum is acknowledged by _____/child/ or as the case may be./

4. *Agreement for benefit of parent only.* On the death of _____/parent/, this agreement shall become null and void, except as to liabilities expressly assumed by _____/child/ hereunder. This agreement is a personal contract for the benefit of _____/parent/ only, and it is not intended to benefit any other person.

In Witness whereof, the parties have executed this agreement at _____/designate place of execution/ the day and year first above written.

/Signatures/

Appendix I

FORM: AGREEMENT BETWEEN PARENT AND CHILD FOR SUPPORT-CONVEYANCE OF REAL PROPERTY AS CONSIDERATION

As consideration for the care and support to be provided by _____/child/, _____/parent/ shall convey to _____/child/ by deed, real property in the County of _____, State of _____, more particularly described as follows: _____/legal description/. The transfer shall take place on _____, 19____. If _____/child/ shall predecease _____/parent/ and shall die within _____ years, _____/parent/ shall receive _____Dollars ($_____) from the estate of _____/child/ as further consideration for the transfer of the real property.

Appendix J

FORM: AGREEMENT BETWEEN PARENT AND CHILD FOR SUPPORT-TRANSFER OF PERSONAL PROPERTY AS CONSIDERATION

As consideration for the support to be provided by _____ /child/, _____ /parent/ shall transfer to _____ /child/ personal property described as follows: _____ /legal description/. This property shall become the separate property of the child on the date of the transfer, _____, 19____.

Appendix K

FORM: AGREEMENT BETWEEN PARENT AND CHILD FOR SUPPORT-PARENT TO PROVIDE FOR CHILD IN WILL AS CONSIDERATION

As consideration for _____/the room and board/ to be provided by _____/child/, _____/parent/ shall provide in /his *or* her/ will that all of the property of _____/parent/ both real and personal, shall pass to _____/child/ on the death of _____/parent/. A copy of the will, including a provision to this effect, is attached to this agreement as Exhibit "_____."

INDEX

A
Alimony
  awards, 20;
  effect of divorce, 16-20;
  jails, 24;
  modification of, 24-25;
  money judgment, 20-21;
  security for future payments, 22-24

B
Bond, as support guarantee, 1-2

C
Child support of parents, 37
Compensation insurance, 46
Compulsory insurance, 46
Community property, 8-11
Custody, 25, 34-35

D
Deserting father, 40-41
Desertion, 1-2
Desertion statutes, 5-6
Divorce, effects of, 15-16
Dower & Curtesy, 5-6

E
Enforcement of support, 2-4

F
Family allowances, 14
Federal Compensation Act, 48
Federal Employers Liability Act, 48
Father's liability for necessaries, 35-36

G
Garnishee, 21

H
Homestead, 13-14

I
Illegitimate children, 37 *et seq.*
Inheritance rights,
  adopted children, 43
  illegitimate children, 42
in loco parentis, 36-37

L
Longshoreman's Act, 48

M
Married Women's Property Acts, 6-8
Mutual Obligation, 4

N
National Desertion Bureau, 3
Necessaries, 5 (See also, Father's liabilities)
NOLEO, 31
Non-support, 6

O
Old Age Insurance, see Social Security Act

P
Parent Locator Service, 32-34
Parental support, 29-31
Paupers, 45

Property rights of wife, 6 (see also, Married Women's Property Acts)

S

Sequestration, 21
Social Security Act,
　Appeals, 6061
　applying for, 60
　Building protection, 52
　Financing of, 58-60
　History of, 49-52
　Monthly check amounts, 52-58
　Outside U.S., 58
Supplementary Security Income, 61-62

U

Uniform Desertion and Non-Support Acts, 5
Uniform Reciprocal Enforcement of Support Act, 4, 31-32
Uniform Support of Dependants Act, 4
Uniform state support laws, 3

W

Workmens' Compensation Laws, 45, *et seq.*

LEGAL ALMANAC SERIES CONVERSION TABLE
List of Present Titles and Authors

1. LAW OF SEPARATION AND DIVORCE, 4th Ed., P.J.T. Callahan
2. HOW TO MAKE A WILL/HOW TO USE TRUSTS, 4th Ed., P.J.T. Callahan
3. LAW OF ADOPTION, 4th Ed., M.I. Leavy & R.D. Weinberg
4. REAL ESTATE LAW FOR HOMEOWNER AND BROKER, P.J.T. Callahan & L.M. Nussbaum
5. ELIGIBILITY FOR ENTRY TO THE U.S., 3rd Ed., R.D. Weinberg
6. LAW OF GUARDIANSHIPS, 3rd Ed., R.V. MacKay
7. LABOR LAW, 3rd Ed., D. Epp
8. HOW TO BECOME A CITIZEN OF THE U.S., 4th Ed., L.F. Jessup
9. SEXUAL CONDUCT AND THE LAW, 2nd Ed., G. Mueller
10. LAW OF CREDIT, 2nd Ed., L.G. Greene
11. LANDLORD AND TENANT, Rev. Ed., L.F. Jessup
12. LAW OF SUPPORT, 3rd Ed., F.H. Kuchler
13. CIVIL LIBERTY AND CIVIL RIGHTS, 6th Ed., E.S. Newman
14. COPYRIGHT, PATENTS, TRADEMARKS, R. Wincor, & I. Mandell
15. LAW OF LIBEL AND SLANDER, 3rd Ed., E.C. Thomas
16. LAWS GOVERNING AMUSEMENTS, R.M. Debevec
17. SCHOOLS AND THE LAW, 4th Ed., E.E. Reutter
18. FAMILY PLANNING AND THE LAW, 2nd Ed., R.D. Weinberg
19. STATE WORKMEN'S COMPENSATION, W.R. Dittmar
20. MEDICARE, S. Goldberger
21. HOW TO SECURE COPYRIGHT, O.P. (See #14)
22. LAW OF JUVENILE JUSTICE, S. Rubin
23. RELIGION, CULTS AND THE LAW, 2nd Ed., A. Burstein
24. ELECTION PROCESS, 2nd Ed., A. Reitman & R.B. Davidson
25. DRIVER'S MANUAL, Rev. Ed., T. Mattern & A.J. Mathes
26. PUBLIC OFFICIALS, H.Y. Bernard
27. ALCOHOL AND DRUG ABUSE AND THE LAW, I.J. Sloan
28. HOW TO PROTECT AND PATENT YOUR INVENTION, O.P. (See #14)
29. LAW FOR THE BUSINESSMAN, B.D. Reams, Jr.
30. PSYCHIATRY, THE LAW, AND MENTAL HEALTH, S. Pearlstein
31. HOW TO SERVE ON A JURY, 2nd Ed., P. Francis
32. CRIMES AND PENALTIES, 2nd Ed., B.R. White
33. LAW OF INHERITANCE, 3rd Ed., E.M. Wypyski
34. CHANGE OF NAME AND LAW OF NAMES, 2nd Ed., E.J. Bander
35. LAW OF ACCIDENTS, W.M. Kunstler
36. LAW OF CONTRACTS, 2nd Ed., R. Wincor
37. LAW OF INSURANCE, 2nd Ed., E.M. Taylor
38. LAW OF PHILANTHROPY, E.S. Newman
39. ARBITRATION PRECEPTS AND PRINCIPLES, C.K. Wehringer
40. THE BILL OF RIGHTS AND THE POLICE, 3rd Ed., M. Zarr
41. LAW OF BUYING AND SELLING, 2nd Ed., B.R. White
42. THE INVESTOR'S LEGAL GUIDE, 2nd Ed., S.I. Kaufman
43. LEGAL STATUS OF LIVING TOGETHER, I.J. Sloan
44. LAW BOOKS FOR NON-LAW LIBRARIES AND LAYMEN, A BIBLIOGRAPHY, R.M. Mersky
45. NEW LIFE STYLE AND THE CHANGING LAW, 2nd Ed., L.F. Jessup
46. YOUTH AND THE LAW, 3rd Ed., I.J. Sloan
47. LAW AND THE SPORTSMAN, R.M. Debevec
48. LAW OF RETIREMENT, 2nd Ed., L.F. Jessup
49. LAW FOR THE PET OWNER, D.S. Edgar
50. INCOME AND ESTATE TAX PLANNING, I.J. Sloan
51. TAX PLANNING, (See #50)
52. LEGAL PROTECTION FOR THE CONSUMER, 2nd Ed., S. Morganstern
53. LEGAL STATUS OF WOMEN, 2nd Ed., P. Francis
54. PRIVACY—ITS LEGAL PROTECTION, 2nd Ed., H. Gross
55. PROTECTION THROUGH THE LAW, 2nd Ed., P. Francis
56. LAW OF ART AND ANTIQUES, S. Hodes
57. LAW OF DEATH AND DISPOSAL OF THE DEAD, 2nd Ed., H.Y. Bernard
58. DICTIONARY OF SELECTED LEGAL TERMS AND MAXIMS, 2nd Ed., E.J. Bander
59. LAW OF ENGAGEMENT AND MARRIAGE, 2nd Ed., F.H. Kuchler
60. CONDEMNATION: YOUR RIGHTS WHEN GOVERNMENT ACQUIRES YOUR PROPERTY, G. Lawrence
61. CONFIDENTIAL AND OTHER PRIVILEGED COMMUNICATIONS, R.D. Weinerg
62. UNDERSTANDING THE UNIFORM COMMERCIAL CODE, D. Lloyd
63. WHEN AND HOW TO CHOOSE AN ATTORNEY, 2nd Ed., C.K. Wehringer
64. LAW OF SELF-DEFENSE, F.S. & J. Baum
65. ENVIRONMENT AND THE LAW, 2nd Ed., I.J. Sloan
66. LEGAL PROTECTION IN GARNISHMENT AND ATTACHMENT, S. Morganstern
67. HOW TO BE A WITNESS, K. Tierney
68. AUTOMOBILE LIABILITY AND THE CHANGING LAW, M.G. Woodroof
69. PENALTIES FOR MISCONDUCT ON THE JOB, A. Avins
70. LEGAL REGULATION OF CONSUMER CREDIT, S. Morganstern
71. RIGHT OF ACCESS TO INFORMATION FROM THE GOVERNMENT, S.D. Thurman
72. COOPERATIVES AND CONDOMINIUMS, P.E. Kehoe
73. RIGHTS OF CONVICTS, H.I. Handman
74. FINDING THE LAW-GUIDE TO LEGAL RESEARCH, D. Lloyd
75. LAWS GOVERNING BANKS AND THEIR CUSTOMERS, S. Mandell
76. HUMAN BODY AND THE LAW, C.L. Levy
77. HOW TO COPE WITH U.S. CUSTOMS, A.I. Demcy

LEGAL ALMANAC SERIES CONVERSION TABLE
List of Present Titles and Authors

1. LAW OF SEPARATION AND DIVORCE, 4th Ed., P.J.T. Callahan
2. HOW TO MAKE A WILL/HOW TO USE TRUSTS, 4th Ed., P.J.T. Callahan
3. LAW OF ADOPTION, 4th Ed., M.I. Leavy & R.D. Weinberg
4. REAL ESTATE LAW FOR HOMEOWNER AND BROKER, P.J.T. Callahan & L.M. Nussbaum
5. ELIGIBILITY FOR ENTRY TO THE U.S., 3rd Ed., R.D. Weinberg
6. LAW OF GUARDIANSHIPS, 3rd Ed., R.V. MacKay
7. LABOR LAW, 3rd Ed., D. Epp
8. HOW TO BECOME A CITIZEN OF THE U.S., 4th Ed., L.F. Jessup
9. SEXUAL CONDUCT AND THE LAW, 2nd Ed., G. Mueller
10. LAW OF CREDIT, 2nd Ed., L.G. Greene
11. LANDLORD AND TENANT, Rev. Ed., L.F. Jessup
12. LAW OF SUPPORT, 3rd Ed., F.H. Kuchler
13. CIVIL LIBERTY AND CIVIL RIGHTS, 6th Ed., E.S. Newman
14. COPYRIGHT, PATENTS, TRADEMARKS, R. Wincor, & I. Mandell
15. LAW OF LIBEL AND SLANDER, 3rd Ed., E.C. Thomas
16. LAWS GOVERNING AMUSEMENTS, R.M. Debevec
17. SCHOOLS AND THE LAW, 4th Ed., E.E. Reutter
18. FAMILY PLANNING AND THE LAW, 2nd Ed., R.D. Weinberg
19. STATE WORKMEN'S COMPENSATION, W.R. Dittmar
20. MEDICARE, S. Goldberger
21. HOW TO SECURE COPYRIGHT, O.P. (See #14)
22. LAW OF JUVENILE JUSTICE, S. Rubin
23. RELIGION, CULTS AND THE LAW, 2nd Ed., A. Burstein
24. ELECTION PROCESS, 2nd Ed., A. Reitman & R.B. Davidson
25. DRIVER'S MANUAL, Rev. Ed., T. Mattern & A.J. Mathes
26. PUBLIC OFFICIALS, H.Y. Bernard
27. ALCOHOL AND DRUG ABUSE AND THE LAW, I.J. Sloan
28. HOW TO PROTECT AND PATENT YOUR INVENTION, O.P. (See #14)
29. LAW FOR THE BUSINESSMAN, B.D. Reams, Jr.
30. PSYCHIATRY, THE LAW, AND MENTAL HEALTH, S. Pearlstein
31. HOW TO SERVE ON A JURY, 2nd Ed., P. Francis
32. CRIMES AND PENALTIES, 2nd Ed., B.R. White
33. LAW OF INHERITANCE, 3rd Ed., E.M. Wypyski
34. CHANGE OF NAME AND LAW OF NAMES, 2nd Ed., E.J. Bander
35. LAW OF ACCIDENTS, W.M. Kunstler
36. LAW OF CONTRACTS, 2nd Ed., R. Wincor
37. LAW OF INSURANCE, 2nd Ed., E.M. Taylor
38. LAW OF PHILANTHROPY, E.S. Newman
39. ARBITRATION PRECEPTS AND PRINCIPLES, C.K. Wehringer
40. THE BILL OF RIGHTS AND THE POLICE, 3rd Ed., M. Zarr
41. LAW OF BUYING AND SELLING, 2nd Ed., B.R. White
42. THE INVESTOR'S LEGAL GUIDE, 2nd Ed., S.I. Kaufman
43. LEGAL STATUS OF LIVING TOGETHER, I.J. Sloan
44. LAW BOOKS FOR NON-LAW LIBRARIES AND LAYMEN, A BIBLIOGRAPHY, R.M. Mersky
45. NEW LIFE STYLE AND THE CHANGING LAW, 2nd Ed., L.F. Jessup
46. YOUTH AND THE LAW, 3rd Ed., I.J. Sloan
47. LAW AND THE SPORTSMAN, R.M. Debevec
48. LAW OF RETIREMENT, 2nd Ed., L.F. Jessup
49. LAW FOR THE PET OWNER, D.S. Edgar
50. INCOME AND ESTATE TAX PLANNING, I.J. Sloan
51. TAX PLANNING, (See #50)
52. LEGAL PROTECTION FOR THE CONSUMER, 2nd Ed., S. Morganstern
53. LEGAL STATUS OF WOMEN, 2nd Ed., P. Francis
54. PRIVACY—ITS LEGAL PROTECTION, 2nd Ed., H. Gross
55. PROTECTION THROUGH THE LAW, 2nd Ed., P. Francis
56. LAW OF ART AND ANTIQUES, S. Hodes
57. LAW OF DEATH AND DISPOSAL OF THE DEAD, 2nd Ed., H.Y. Bernard
58. DICTIONARY OF SELECTED LEGAL TERMS AND MAXIMS, 2nd Ed., E.J. Bander
59. LAW OF ENGAGEMENT AND MARRIAGE, 2nd Ed., F.H. Kuchler
60. CONDEMNATION: YOUR RIGHTS WHEN GOVERNMENT ACQUIRES YOUR PROPERTY, G. Lawrence
61. CONFIDENTIAL AND OTHER PRIVILEGED COMMUNICATIONS, R.D. Weinerg
62. UNDERSTANDING THE UNIFORM COMMERCIAL CODE, D. Lloyd
63. WHEN AND HOW TO CHOOSE AN ATTORNEY, 2nd Ed., C.K. Wehringer
64. LAW OF SELF-DEFENSE, F.S. & J. Baum
65. ENVIRONMENT AND THE LAW, 2nd Ed., I.J. Sloan
66. LEGAL PROTECTION IN GARNISHMENT AND ATTACHMENT, S. Morganstern
67. HOW TO BE A WITNESS, K. Tierney
68. AUTOMOBILE LIABILITY AND THE CHANGING LAW, M.G. Woodroof
69. PENALTIES FOR MISCONDUCT ON THE JOB, A. Avins
70. LEGAL REGULATION OF CONSUMER CREDIT, S. Morganstern
71. RIGHT OF ACCESS TO INFORMATION FROM THE GOVERNMENT, S.D. Thurman
72. COOPERATIVES AND CONDOMINIUMS, P.E. Kehoe
73. RIGHTS OF CONVICTS, H.I. Handman
74. FINDING THE LAW-GUIDE TO LEGAL RESEARCH, D. Lloyd
75. LAWS GOVERNING BANKS AND THEIR CUSTOMERS, S. Mandell
76. HUMAN BODY AND THE LAW, C.L. Levy
77. HOW TO COPE WITH U.S. CUSTOMS, A.I. Demcy

LEGAL ALMANAC SERIES CONVERSION TABLE
List of Original Titles and Authors

1. LAW OF MARRIAGE AND DIVORCE, R.V. MacKay
2. HOW TO MAKE A WILL SIMPLIFIED, P.J.T. Callahan
3. LAW OF ADOPTION, M.L. Leavy
4. LAW OF REAL ESTATE, P.J.T. Callahan
5. IMMIGRATION LAWS OF THE UNITED STATES, C.M. Crosswell
6. GUARDIANSHIP LAW, R.V. MacKay
7. LABOR LAW, C. Rachlin
8. HOW TO BECOME A CITIZEN OF THE U.S., Margaret E. Hall
9. SEX AND THE STATUTORY LAW, Part I, R.V. Sherwin
9a. SEX AND THE STATUTORY LAW, Part II, R.V. Sherwin
10. LAW OF DEBTOR AND CREDITOR, L.G. Greene
11. LANDLORD AND TENANT, F.H. Kuchler
12. LAW OF SUPPORT, F.H. Kuchler
13. CIVIL RIGHTS AND CIVIL LIBERTIES, E.S. Newman
14. LAW OF NOTARIES PUBLIC, L.G. Greene
15. LAW OF LIBEL AND SLANDER, E.C. Thomas
16. LIQUOR LAWS, B.M. Bernard
17. EDUCATION LAW, D.T. Marke
18. LAW OF MISSING PEOPLE, F. Fraenkel
19. STATE WORKMEN'S COMPENSATION, W.R. Dittmar
20. LAW OF MEDICINE, P.J.T. Callahan
21. HOW TO SECURE COPYRIGHT, R. Wincor
22. JUVENILE DELINQUENCY, F.B. Sussman
23. LAWS CONCERNING RELIGION, A. Burstein
24. ELECTION LAWS, B.M. Bernard
25. DRIVER'S MANUAL, T. Mattern & A.J. Mathes
26. STATE SOCIAL SECURITY LAWS, S.H. Asch
27. MANUAL OF CIVIL AVIATION LAW, T. Mattern & A.J. Mathes
28. HOW TO PROTECT AND PATENT YOUR INVENTION, I. Mandell
29. LAW FOR THE SMALL BUSINESSMAN, M.L. Leavy
30. INSANITY LAWS, W.R. Dittmar
31. HOW TO SERVE ON A JURY, P. Francis
32. CRIMES AND PENALTIES, T.B. Stuchiner
33. LAW OF INHERITANCE, E.M. Wypyski
34. HOW TO CHANGE YOUR NAME, L.G. Greene
35. LAW OF ACCIDENTS, W.M. Kunstler
36. LAW OF CONTRACTS, R. Wincor
37. LAW OF INSURANCE, I.M. Taylor
38. LAW OF PHILANTHROPY, E.S. Newman
39. LAW OF SELLING, J.A. Hoehlein
40. LAW OF PERSONAL LIBERTIES, R. Schwartzmann
41. LAW OF BUYING AND SELLING, B.R. White
42. PRACTICAL AND LEGAL MANUAL FOR THE INVESTOR, S.I. Kaufman
43. LAW FOR THE HOMEOWNER, REAL ESTATE OPERATOR, AND BROKER, L.M. Nussbaum
44. LAW FOR THE TOURIST, R.J. DeSeife
45. LAW FOR THE FAMILY MAN, L.F. Jessup
46. LEGAL STATUS OF YOUNG ADULTS, P.J.T. Callahan
47. LAW AND THE SPORTSMAN, R.M. Debevec
48. LAW OF RETIREMENT, L.F. Jessup
49. LAW FOR THE PET OWNER, D.S. Edgar
50. ESTATE PLANNING, P.J. Goldberg
51. TAX PLANNING, P.J. Goldberg
52. LEGAL PROTECTION FOR THE CONSUMER, S. Morganstern
53. LEGAL STATUS OF WOMEN, P. Francis
54. PRIVACY—ITS LEGAL PROTECTION, H. Gross
55. PROTECTION THROUGH THE LAW, P. Francis
56. LAW OF ART AND ANTIQUES, S. Hodes
57. LAW OF DEATH AND DISPOSAL OF THE DEAD, H.Y. Bernard
58. LAW DICTIONARY OF PRACTICAL DEFINITIONS, E.J. Bander
59. LAW OF ENGAGEMENT AND MARRIAGE, F.H. Kuchler
60. CONDEMNATION: YOUR RIGHTS WHEN GOVERNMENT ACQUIRES YOUR PROPERTY, G. Lawrence
61. CONFIDENTIAL AND OTHER PRIVILEGED COMMUNICATION, R.D. Weinberg
62. UNDERSTANDING THE UNIFORM COMMERCIAL CODE, D. Lloyd
63. WHEN AND HOW TO CHOOSE AN ATTORNEY, C.K. Wehringer
64. LAW OF SELF-DEFENSE, F.S. & J. Baum
65. ENVIRONMENT AND THE LAW, I.J. Sloan
66. LEGAL PROTECTION IN GARNISHMENT AND ATTACHMENT, S. Morganstern
67. HOW TO BE A WITNESS, K.Tierney
68. AUTOMOBILE LIABILITY AND THE CHANGING LAW, M.G. Woodroof
69. PENALTIES FOR MISCONDUCT ON THE JOB, A. Avins
70. LEGAL REGULATION OF CONSUMER CREDIT, S. Morganstern
71. RIGHT OF ACCESS TO INFORMATION FROM THE GOVERNMENT, S.D. Thurman
72. COOPERATIVES AND CONDOMINIUMS, P.E. Kehoe
73. RIGHTS OF CONVICTS, H.I. Handman
74. FINDING THE LAW-GUIDE TO LEGAL RESEARCH, D. Lloyd
75. LAWS GOVERNING BANKS AND THEIR CUSTOMERS, S. Mandell
76. HUMAN BODY AND THE LAW, C.L. Levy
77. HOW TO COPE WITH U.S. CUSTOMS, A.I. Demcy